BETWEEN THE TIDES
in Washington and Oregon

RYAN P. KELLY,
TERRIE KLINGER & JOHN J. MEYER

BETWEEN THE TIDES

in Washington and Oregon

EXPLORING BEACHES
AND TIDEPOOLS

UNIVERSITY OF WASHINGTON PRESS

SEATTLE

A Ruth Kirk Book

Between the Tides in Washington and Oregon was published with the assistance of a grant from the Ruth Kirk Book Fund, which supports publications that inform the general public on the history, natural history, archaeology, and Native cultures of the Pacific Northwest.

This book was also made possible in part by a generous gift from Suzanne Ragen, in memory of Brooks Ragen.

Additional support was provided by the Samuel and Althea Stroum Endowed Book Fund.

Design by Derek George / Composition and layout by Doug Goewey
Composed in Ashbury, typeface designed by Dieter Hofrichter

26 25 24 23 22   5 4 3 2 1

Printed and bound in China

Photographs by the authors unless otherwise noted.

UNIVERSITY OF WASHINGTON PRESS
uwapress.uw.edu

LIBRARY OF CONGRESS CATALOGING-IN-PUBLICATION DATA
Names: Kelly, Ryan P. (Ryan Patrick), author. | Klinger, Terrie, 1956– author.
Title: Between the tides in Washington and Oregon : exploring beaches and tidepools / Ryan P. Kelly, Terrie Klinger, and John J. Meyer.
Description: Seattle : University of Washington Press, [2022] | Includes index.
Identifiers: LCCN 2021034648 (print) | LCCN 2021034649 (ebook)
  | ISBN 9780295749952 (hardcover) | ISBN 9780295749969 (paperback)
  | ISBN 9780295749976 (ebook)
Subjects: LCSH: Coastal ecology–Washington (State)–Guidebooks. | Coastal ecology–Oregon–Guidebooks.
Classification: LCC QH105.W2 K45 2022 (print) | LCC QH105.W2 (ebook)
  | DDC 577.5/109797–dc23
LC record available at https://lccn.loc.gov/2021034648
LC ebook record available at https://lccn.loc.gov/2021034649

♾ This paper meets the requirements of ANSI/NISO Z39.48-1992 (Permanence of Paper).

For the very curious, in particular the ones I live with
—RYAN KELLY

For all my teachers, and especially Paul Dayton
and Rob DeWreede, with deep appreciation
—TERRIE KLINGER

For Adrienne, whose love for the ocean
and its creatures is boundless
—JOHN MEYER

CONTENTS

BETWEEN THE TIDES
in Washington and Oregon

The sun sets on the Washington coast at Second Beach, Olympic National Park.

INTRODUCTION

You can tell what people love by what they do in their free time: musicians, after hours, playing together in empty rooms; chefs cooking for one another. Those drawn to the shore are the same. Break time at a meeting of marine biologists will find many facedown on the rocks, surveying and exclaiming—a busman's holiday.

What draws us to the coast? A sense of dynamism and forces larger than us, perhaps. Or a human urge to see the edge of things. The coast lets us peek under the rug of a different world.

It's captivating, in part, because it hints at very different ways of being alive on this planet. And yet it's easily accessible. We can often walk or drive to get there. Power, beauty, mystery, and enchantment are an intoxicating mix for locals and the most casual visitor alike.

Some lucky people go to the shore for a living. Of these, a few have the privilege to study the coastline and write about it. We count ourselves among these few.

We hope to capture that sense of bottomless curiosity, aesthetic and scientific attraction, and even adventure. This is an easy sell; the US West Coast already gets millions of visitors each year. But like many things, the shoreline becomes far more interesting as you learn more about it. Our real goal, then, is to uncover some of the hidden workings of the coast, to show why the shore near Seattle, Washington, is different from the shore near Astoria, Oregon. Building up a sense of how the coast works—which creatures live where, and why—deepens our sense of wonder and gives us more reasons to keep coming back.

Ecology is the study of what lives where, and why. It is the search to reveal the processes behind the patterns we see in the living world. Of course, this undertaking assumes that we have noticed patterns in the living world in the first place. Some of these are obvious: tropical plants don't grow well in Seattle, for example, and freshwater fish don't live in the ocean. But many more subtle patterns surround us. And moreover, do we ever ask about what drives these patterns, whether they're obvious or not?

We go to the beach and we see various plants and animals living on the rocks in the surf zone, but rarely do we wonder why they live in one place and not another. It's not trivial to ask why a particular snail lives under a rock, but a limpet lives on top of the same rock. Or why you see barnacles even at high tide, but only the lowest tide exposes many of the sea stars, brittle stars, and the like. We can ask the same question at a larger scale as well: why, for instance, does one sea star live in northern California and Oregon, while a different one lives in southern California and Baja California? These are some of the questions that have fascinated ecologists since before the discipline had a name.

This book is about *why*, rather than *what*. It's about process, rather than merely the patterns those processes create. Taken this way, a day at the shore becomes a detective's adventure, with each species found there signifying something about the environmental conditions and the other species present. A mussel shell lying on the sand isn't just scenery—it's a clue: it means mussels live here or nearby. Which mussel is it? Knowing something about this tells you whether conditions tend to be calm or rough. Is the shell whole or fragmented? This might tell you about how the mussel was dislodged or eaten. If the shell is whole, does it have a small hole drilled into it? If so, that's probably a mark of a predatory snail (which also must live nearby; the shape of that hole can tell you which species of snail). Is there anything growing on the mussel shell? Barnacles, small tube worms, algae, et cetera? More clues about the conditions at the site.

It is great fun to recognize living creatures as you walk through the world. For many, this can be like seeing old friends, and it lends a sense of place and belonging and connection. But even more deeply, if each living element in a location is a clue about the inner workings of the world, learning about just a few species can spark a durable inquisitive flame. This kind of inquiry, this worldview, is what ecology is all about.

Ecologists hope to learn relatively simple rules by which the riotous complexity of life takes shape. Evolution by natural selection generates the species in existence, generally over long time spans. Then, at shorter timescales, these species arrange themselves in space and time according to the rules of ecology.

Comparing adjacent sites along the shore is an opportunity for ecological inference. Given what we suppose are the same starting conditions and species, what forces yield different communities at the adjacent sites? We cannot know for certain; we are observing a work in progress and inferring its machinations. But just as a baker may infer both the ingredients and the process that result in a loaf of bread, ecologists make educated guesses about the ways in which today's species assemblages came to exist.

But bread has just a few ingredients, while an ecological community may have thousands, each one affecting the whole. We therefore look for shortcuts to pare down this complexity somewhat, creating manageable units without missing anything important. For purposes of this book, we often do so by lumping closely related species together (e.g., "limpets," which might be ten or more individual species, each with a similar, but not identical, ecological role). Other common simplifying techniques include grouping by ecological "guilds" (e.g., grazing species, filter feeders, etc.), or by trophic level (photosynthesizer, primary consumer, etc.).

However, these details need not trouble the reader too much. The point is that ecologists find great and challenging beauty in complexity arising out of simplicity.

This book is a relatively compact tool readers might use to better understand and appreciate any visit to the coast. We aim at the nonexpert, and the ideas we bring together—drawn from ecology, biology, and related fields—apply to coastlines worldwide, even if we have focused on Washington and Oregon here.

Accordingly, we set out general information in the first two chapters, describing the field on which coastal ecology plays out, first dealing with nonliving parts and then the living ones. We then apply these concepts by featuring selected coastal sites in chapters 3–6. We have arranged these latter chapters geographically from north to south, with the idea that this book might be handy in the car on a road trip or otherwise during visits to parts of the coastline. In highlighting particular sites within each chapter, we have organized them from north to south, too, and attempted to cover interesting or distinctive examples of larger concepts.

In general, sites we've included are areas that people are likely to visit but that also illustrate core ecological concepts. Note that there are many other sites along the coast that illustrate the same points. To avoid giving redundant information, we cross-reference chapters to highlight ideas or places or species discussed elsewhere, and we refer back to the first two chapters for explanation and context where the connection is not readily apparent.

The Further Reading list and the index are also indispensable tools for finding specific information. We've included good references for additional reading and have prepared an exhaustive index to provide many points of access for this book itself.

For a few reasons, we have not set out to write a definitive guide to every beach and headland along the West Coast of the continental US. First, such a book would be hopelessly large and detailed, far more than readers would want to lug around (more than 1,500 miles of coastline would call for repetitive information on similar habitats and landforms). Second, the book would be out of date the moment we finished it; as shown in the chapters that follow, the ecology of the West Coast is quite dynamic. Third, many good books already exist to give readers specific guidance on how best to reach the local shoreline and which species they might see once they arrive. We have listed some such books in Further Reading.

Similarly, this book is not an exhaustive guide to every species visitors might hope to see along the shore. Here again, many such books already exist and several are included in Further Reading, but more broadly, we have tried to focus on the *why* of coastal ecology, rather than the *what*. We have given our attention to the most common, compelling, or illustrative species at different sites, knowing full well that much more diversity exists than we would want to try to cover here. Though many of these species occur at multiple sites along the West Coast—or, indeed, along the entire coastline—we describe them in the chapter where they are perhaps best known or most iconic or most often seen, in phylogenetic order. And wherever possible, we include the scientific as well as the common name for the flora and fauna we describe, though sometimes we provide just a genus, family, or order for groups of species or ecological guilds.

This book focuses on Washington and Oregon, which are part of a larger marine ecosystem that extends from British Columbia to California. Throughout this region, ecological transitions occur from north to south. Even so, in the context of this large marine ecosystem, the flora and fauna are fairly consistent throughout maritime Washington and Oregon. The species assemblages in the tidepools of southern Oregon resemble those in northern Washington, the coastal vegetation zones are similar, and so on. The overall faunal similarity within Washington and Oregon gives us license to focus on the smaller details that drive local patterns. The creatures found in sheltered coves are quite different from those on exposed coasts, for example, and the habitats of sand-covered shores are radical departures from those along rocky headlands nearby. Zooming in on differences within a faunal region lets us highlight ecological patterns that would otherwise get lost, giving a more detailed sense of what lives where and why.

In starting to think about what lives where, and why, it might be helpful to think about where you live, and why. Perhaps you were born where you presently live; maybe you came from elsewhere. How were you transported, and for what reason? Maybe you moved because you have a particular way of making a living, and you needed a place that would let you do that. Perhaps you just liked the weather, or you couldn't get along with your old neighbors. Maybe you would move again if you could, but you face some constraints. Maybe you have children, and there is some tension between what is good for you and what is good for them. In the end, there are trade-offs between all of these factors—and many others—but each factor is intimately tied to place and time: where you live is inextricably a product of your personal history and your social

Geographic regions covered by chapters 3 through 6: Washington's Puget Sound and greater Salish Sea (chapter 3), Washington's outer coast (chapter 4), the northern Oregon Coast (chapter 5), and the southern Oregon coast (chapter 6).

and ecological situation. The trade-offs would be different if you lived in another place or time.

And so it is with every living creature. Each faces a variety of constraints; each is the product of history and happenstance.

In this vein, developing an appreciation for ecology requires developing a sense of place and time. What makes this place different from that one is both a cause and an effect of the species that live there and of the processes leading up to this point in time.

Change is a recurring theme of this book. Over timescales ranging from hours to millions of years, coastlines are some of the more dynamic environments on the planet. Our approach to such change is explicit: in any location, the beach you see will be different, in subtle or major ways, from the beach we have seen. Time and tide will influence the species you see, abundance will wax and wane in response to season or year, ocean conditions will vary, and a warming planet will reset tenuous balances that now exist. Tomorrow, the beach will be different than it is today.

Perennial change is a persistent feature, in particular, of the thin line between land and sea, but these changes aren't random. Many occur along predictable axes, and by developing a deeper sense of how the world works and why, we learn to better "read" conditions on the ground. Although the specifics will necessarily shift over time, the ecological concepts we set out in this book will remain useful for understanding what lives where and why. And despite constant change, the shore will remain a source of deep interest and inspiration for all of us.

When we started out to write this book, we asked ourselves, Might we be doing more harm than good here, encouraging people to visit beautiful habitats that could be damaged by visitation? Our answer is that, by helping visitors understand and appreciate the natural world, we can both encourage and protect. We hope to inspire a sense of collective responsibility to preserve these habitats for future generations and for the sake of their own intrinsic worth.

As far as we are aware, the first detailed English-language narrative of life along the shore is Philip Henry Gosse's *A Naturalist's Rambles on the Devonshire Coast*, from 1853. Even then, when the world's population was less than one-sixth of today's, Gosse encountered the English shore in the wake of the industrial revolution and subject to human pressures of all sorts. And half a century later, Gosse's son referred (in his 1907 *Father and Son*) to the English shore as having been "ravaged" by collectors, "crushed under the rough paw of well-meaning, idle-minded curiosity" in the intervening years; the classic *Between Pacific Tides* by Edward Ricketts and others (see Further Reading) recounts the Gosses' experiences as a lesson for readers of the mid-twentieth century.

Perhaps people are always inclined to view ecosystems of the past as unspoiled relative to today's, but we have good evidence to the contrary. Environmental stewardship has made great strides in the past half century, with tangible results. In the western US, the air and water are far cleaner than they were a generation ago. Whales have returned in significant numbers to Puget Sound and elsewhere along the coast; kelp forests and otters have returned to Monterey Bay, California, resurrecting both the local ecosystem and the local economy. Bald eagles and brown pelicans are once again common. These and many other examples are great and important successes. If we do not appreciate them as such every day, it is because people quickly adjust to their surroundings and, in many cases, quickly forget the day-to-day experiences of the past. Ecologists refer to this as the *shifting baseline* problem: because the world is always changing around us, we tend to keep resetting our idea of "normal" to match present conditions.

In sum, naturalists of every era encounter a world changed by their predecessors. But this need not mean a constant vector of decline in the state of the world's ecosystems. And indeed, we hope and believe that better understanding the places people visit is a likely means of improving stewardship of those places.

1

The Oregon coast

THE TUMULTUOUS EARTH

The deepest mechanics of the planet are unstable: continents collide, ice ages come and go, and large-scale climate changes with the centuries. Because of the slower timescales of most of these changes, they aren't always obvious in everyday life. But the planet's history and inner workings affect the coastal ecology of today, often going a long way toward explaining what lives where, and why.

One example will illustrate this point.

Not too long ago, geologically speaking, Seattle sat under thousands of feet of ice. This fact is central to the story of life in the Pacific Northwest, but it is hard to get your head around. There is the simple matter of height: the ice was about five and a half times the height of Seattle's Space Needle, well taller than any building now on earth. But there is also the matter of mass: such an ice sheet is sufficiently heavy to depress whole portions of a continent. And as it moves, the ice sheet carves fjords and valleys, and upon receding, it litters huge boulders (entertainingly called erratics) about, picked up in its earlier glacial wanderings. Even more astonishingly, as the ice trails away the continent bounces back upward, as if stretching after a ten-thousand-year nap.

Nothing larger than a microbe can live under these thick blankets of ice. Even so, some larger organisms were likely able to survive in pockets referred to as glacial refugia—that is, areas just beyond the reach of the ice sheet that were at least marginally hospitable to macroscopic life. As the glaciers ebbed, species recolonized ice-free areas. This cycle of glacial extinction followed by recolonization likely happened several times during the Pleistocene epoch, which means that everything we see when we visit this part of the world has shown up since the last ice age, invading at a snail's pace across the landscape and seascape. Life in tidepools is no exception. Geneticists, for example, can clearly see which (southern) populations of crabs and clams and fish survived to reinvade northern areas postglaciation, because northern populations are new enough that they haven't had time to build up genetic diversity. They *just* got there, geologically speaking.

LONGER-TERM EARTH PROCESSES

What caused the glaciers to expand and contract?

Periodic changes in the way the earth revolves around the sun mean that some millennia are cooler than others. Ice builds up in the cooler millennia and breaks down as the climate warms. These cycles are excellent examples of small changes at cosmic scales (who knew the tilt of the earth could change over time?) that have enormous effects at ecological scales on the ground—such as burying a continent in a massive slab of ice. And of course these changes directly affect humans, too: without glaciation and climate cycling, humans might never have left Africa and spread out across the world by land.

The planetary counterpoint to glaciation is melting, with the consequent rise and fall of sea level. All of that ice was made of water, and all of that water had to come from somewhere. In a glacial period, there is simply less ocean, and so sea level can be lower by hundreds of vertical feet. What we see as islands today may have been headlands and peninsulas during an ice age. A strait may in fact have been a valley. New Guinea may simply have been more Australia, and Russia and Alaska may have been holding hands, separating the Arctic Ocean from the Pacific for thousands of years at a stretch.

And so, life along the Pacific Ocean teaches us that nature is dynamic: tectonic faults reshape the coast over geological time; new species arise, interact with others, and eventually die out; and the climate is ever-changing, shifting the windows of temperature and habitat that individual species find acceptable. And this is to say nothing of the humans that have come to dominate the coast over the past 15,000 years, whether hunting and gathering along the waterfront, exploiting the nearshore mammals for their fur, or raising skyscrapers at the shore.

With our short life spans, we get to see only a small time-slice of the vast drama that defines Pacific coastal life: that's why we often think of the natural world as a monolithic, constant "other." We tend to assume that the plants and animals we see out there today are the ones that have always been there and that they've always been in the same place. As it turns out, this isn't at all true. On the contrary, rocks and species and ecosystems are samples plucked from a narrative in progress, telling a sometimes-long story of their origins and adventures. Each scene is a product of ancient forces still in progress.

Each visit to the shore helps develop a sense of place and time, growing the knowledge that today is a consequence of an ocean's worth of yesterdays, the idea that *here and now* is inseparable from *there and then*.

BINS OF TIME

Because our personal experiences span relatively limited time frames, it is difficult to think in terms of deeper time. It's easy to let a thousand years and a million years seem like the same irrelevant numbers: our brains tend to round them off to something approximating "far longer than I've been around." (For those who aren't used to working with these very different timescales, it can lead to confusion: one of the authors once got into an argument with a good friend from Bogotá who, when it was suggested that she comes from a different continent, pointed out that North America and South America are conjoined, and there's no reason to treat them separately. That co-author replied that the two continents have been touching for only three million years. Both felt they had won the argument.)

A useful way of learning to zoom in and out through different timescales while looking at, say, a beach, is to create "bins" of time as mental shortcuts. Biologists do this as a matter of course, using terms like *ecological time* (which might encompass weeks to seasons to decades to perhaps thousands of years), *evolutionary time* (referring to hundreds of thousands to millions of years), and *geological time* (which is anything longer than millions of years). This kind of shorthand lets us ignore particular dates or counts of years and instead focus on rough estimates of time in a way that remains quite helpful for appreciating the different processes that have led up to the present day.

The rocks, the sand, the rivers of the West Coast have stories to tell, and in this region, those stories are spectacular. We need not get bogged down by specific dates or even by a decimal place or two. Simply understanding the changes that have occurred over time, and how one change was followed by another and another, helps to deepen our sense of place.

HIGHLIGHTS OF DEEP HISTORY: SHAPING WASHINGTON'S AND OREGON'S COASTS

A few vignettes of the region's deeper history are well worth keeping in mind when adventuring around the coasts of the Pacific Northwest. These examples show the kind of truly monumental events that underlie the present, adding a layer of wonder and appreciation for those already interested in the world around us.

Looking back in deep geological time, hundreds of millions of years ago, most of today's West Coast simply didn't exist. The landmasses today that are home to most of the region's people—western Washington, Oregon, and California—were for millions of years Pacific seabed on a collision course with North America. Over the course of mind-bendingly long periods of time, blocks of rock accumulated along the West Coast as tectonic plates collided with one another, eventually shaping the landmass as we currently know it. In Washington and Oregon, in fact, this collision between plates is still happening, which is why the Pacific Northwest's volcanoes remain active, while California's are long-dormant. Oceanic crust, crushed and melted under the North American continent, fuels the Cascadian volcanoes.

By a few tens of millions of years ago, still squarely in the bin of geological time, the major pieces of Washington and Oregon were in place. But this merely set the stage for more recent dramas to play out.

Stepping far forward in time, to today, rocky outcroppings punctuate the sandy coast of Oregon between the Columbia River and Yaquina Head, just north of Newport. This picturesque collection of sea stacks and headlands is the result of a series of volcanic eruptions, each filling a succession of ancient Columbia River valleys with lava, each extending a finger into the Pacific, and each nudging the Columbia into a different course. Repeated lava flows between seventeen and seven million years ago landed the Columbia in its present location and yielded the capes of northern and central Oregon, vestiges of inland eruptions. Let's think of this (remarkable) set of events as happening in evolutionary time, while recognizing the everyday ecological significance of these headlands: they are the rocks upon which much of the coastal flora and fauna depend, the capes we visit when we go to the shore. Washington has no such volcanic headlands along its outer coast.

Much of the more recent and ecologically relevant history in the region has been dominated by ice. The glaciers retreated at the end of the last ice age, between 15,000 and 13,000 years ago, and thus a hundred times more recently than the lava flows that moved the Columbia. During this interval, at least dozens of truly cataclysmic floods tore through the Columbia River valley, as ice dams holding back ice-age Lake Missoula repeatedly collapsed and re-formed. This ancient lake was enormous, stretching from present-day Missoula, Montana, across the Idaho panhandle nearly to Spokane, Washington. These massive floods emptied the ancient lake across southern Washington and Oregon, discharging water at a rate up to thirteen times that of the present-day Amazon River and transporting cubic miles of earth downstream into the Pacific. The Missoula Floods, as these are known, happened in ecological time, recently enough that humans might well have been around to witness them. Most of today's coastal species were here, too, for these floods, and to the extent that the floods reshaped the mouth of the Columbia and its sands, the floods continue to influence what lives where along the coast.

In this same bin of ecological time, the ice sheets that had covered much of North America retreated far to the north, opening a landscape that has supported humans and tens of thousands of other species ever since. And it's worth noting that in terms of biological evolution, the ice ages are still quite shallow. The average species persists for something like a million years. So even if ice ages aren't in the memory of individuals living now, species that exist at present nearly all were exposed to ice ages in the past, and no doubt they changed in the process.

Today, in the shallowest bin of time, the Olympic Mountains continue to rise, still rebounding after being relieved of the burden of ice sheets in the last glaciation. This mountainous rebound is geological history in the making, as are the eruption of Mount St. Helens, major earthquakes, and tsunamis.

Earthquakes can lift the coastal zone in places, thrusting formerly submerged habitat above sea level, resetting the intertidal zone and likely killing the previous residents. This happens with some regularity around the Pacific Rim: examples come from Chile, Mexico, northern California, Alaska, Japan, New Zealand, and other places where one tectonic plate is being forced beneath another.

Parts of the Washington and Oregon coasts, however, seem to have the opposite response to tectonic activity. Earthquakes in recent geological history—the most recent about 300 years ago—have driven the coast lower relative to sea level, drowning the existing intertidal zones, low-lying forests, and sites of coastal human settlements along with them.

So in a very real way, the past is not past. Ongoing, earth-scale changes shape life along the coast for humans and for every other species that lives here. And developing the most basic sense of the sequence of geological events gives visitors to the coast a powerful lens through which to appreciate the goings-on. That is, the visitor will have developed a sense of place and time that will reveal the coast to be an even more fascinating place than it had seemed at first.

OCEANOGRAPHIC AND EARTH PROCESSES

Highlights of the planet's behavior help to identify common causes behind an astonishingly broad set of patterns. For example, things as

SEA STACKS

No photograph of the rugged Northwest coast is complete without sea stacks, fragments of coast that seem the very embodiments of durability in the face of adversity. And in many respects, this symbolism is fitting: what we see as sea stacks are surviving pieces of earlier coastlines, bits of more-resistant rock that are left behind as less-durable surrounding rock erodes into the waves.

There is a feedback loop to this process: as a resistant chunk of rock begins to emerge out of a cliff side, it forms a headland. Headlands, in turn, are magnets for wave energy as ocean waves refract to hit along both of its flanks, which therefore more quickly erodes the connection between headland and cliff side. The result, after a time, is a sea stack. The timeline for this process can be quite short, both underscoring the dynamic nature of ocean shores and somewhat undercutting sea stacks as symbols of durability.

The Oregon coast is a mix of softer sedimentary rocks and harder volcanic rocks, and hence, a wealth of sea stacks are associated with its rocky headlands. Cannon Beach's Haystack Rock and Pacific City's Chief Kiawanda Rock are iconic examples.

Sea stacks, common on the Washington and Oregon coasts, are reminders of the geological past and of how dynamic the shape of shorelines can be.

different as coastal fog and fish abundance are both linked to ocean processes, which in turn are shaped by earth processes that have forged the landscape and seascape before us.

Tectonics and Subduction

North America's Pacific coast is vastly different from its Atlantic cousin. The Pacific coast is far more dynamic, for one: as the Pacific plate smashes into the North American plate, the heavier ocean crust is driven under the lighter continental crust in the Pacific Northwest. *Smashing* really is the right word for what happens, as entire continents collide with enough force, in the fullness of time, to make seabeds into the planet's highest peaks. It's an unimaginable amount of force—but it happens slowly. The result is the slow accumulation of land that has become the western states over the past 200 million years and the deep, cold water right off the western shores.

The Pacific coast is an active margin, a location where tectonic plates collide, creating earthquakes and raising mountains in the bargain (see figure below). The mountains influence regional weather patterns, and weather patterns influence life along the shore for humans and everything else that lives here.

By contrast, the Atlantic coast is a passive margin, consisting of a broad, sandy shelf stretching for miles out to sea. And here too, *passive* is the correct word: for half a billion years, the Appalachian Mountains have been eroding into sand.

These geological contexts are the settings in which coastal life happens. While the West Coast has many and varied habitats, the habitats of the East Coast are fairly consistent between Cape Cod, Massachusetts, and Florida: mainly sand, mainly flat. Over evolutionary time, more diverse habitats trigger the evolution of more diverse suites of species. It's quite likely, then, that the ecology of the West Coast has been considerably more diverse than the East Coast for millions of years.

Continental plates move great distances over geologic time but average only inches per human lifetime, which is why we think of landmasses as being static, most of the time. But the dynamic nature of continental

TWO TYPES OF CONTINENTAL MARGINS

ACTIVE MARGIN — US WEST COAST
- subduction zones offshore
- vulcanism on land

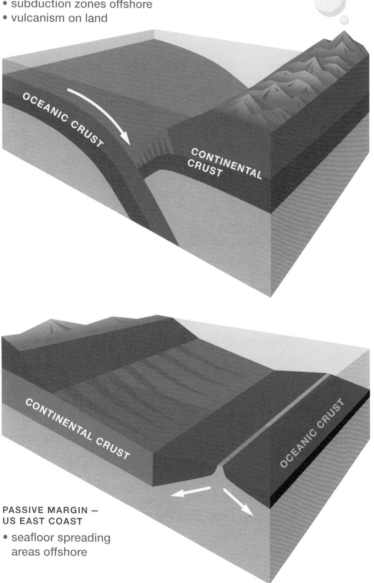

OCEANIC CRUST

CONTINENTAL CRUST

CONTINENTAL CRUST

OCEANIC CRUST

PASSIVE MARGIN — US EAST COAST
- seafloor spreading areas offshore

The arrangement of tectonic plates influences everything from mountains to weather to biodiversity. Plate boundaries along the West Coast of North America (top) make it an active margin, in contrast to the passive margin of the continent's East Coast (bottom).

plates over very long periods of time has created the conditions that we observe, and live in, every day.

The deep ocean water just off the West Coast's shores causes big differences in temperature between land and sea during the daytime, which in turn creates predictable local wind patterns and coastal fog. At a larger scale, prevailing winds tend to blow toward the south along the West Coast, causing coastal upwelling (see figure below) and in turn fueling entire food webs. And finally, we owe to plate tectonics most of our rocky substrates, without which we would not have the diversity of intertidal species that have evolved in place over tens of millions of years.

From San Francisco's fog to the impressive primary productivity feeding schools of fish and the things that prey on them, to the number of marine species living along the West Coast, these (and many more phenomena) all can be traced back to the action of plate tectonics. That is, if the dynamic history of the Pacific shore were knit in a single piece, tugging on the end that is "now" could unravel things all the way back to the forces that have shaped the earth's crust.

The Coriolis Effect: As the World Turns

Under just about all normal circumstances, it is perfectly safe to ignore the fact that we all live on a giant rotating ball. The earth rotates at an essentially constant speed, so there is no acceleration and we don't feel as if we're moving. Instead, the sun appears to be moving. Hence, our language around these facts–"the sun sets"–and hence it took centuries to convince the average person that we–and not the sun–are in motion relative to the rest of the solar system.

However, in some contexts our existence on a rotating ball becomes highly relevant. An airplane pilot leaving Seattle and aiming at Miami, Florida, for example, would land in the Atlantic if the flight path weren't adjusted for the fact that the earth is rotating under the plane while it is in the air. Atmospheric and ocean currents, too, are subject to the same dynamic: physics dictates they move in a straight line, but the earth is continually rotating beneath them. To an outside observer, the result is that their paths appear to curve–to the right, in the northern hemisphere.

CORIOLIS EFFECT

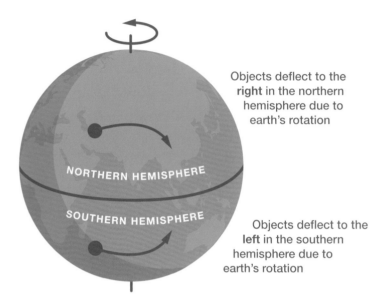

Objects deflect to the **right** in the northern hemisphere due to earth's rotation

NORTHERN HEMISPHERE

SOUTHERN HEMISPHERE

Objects deflect to the **left** in the southern hemisphere due to earth's rotation

The Coriolis effect is a feature of life on a rotating globe; throwing a ball while on a moving merry-go-round is a good small-scale approximation of the same idea. Moving objects appear to deflect to the right (in the northern hemisphere) or left (in the southern hemisphere), with profound consequences for ocean circulation, weather, and climate.

This apparent curvature of the paths of things in motion is called the Coriolis effect. And because air and water are in constant motion across the surface of the spinning earth, we need to account for Coriolis force when we think about air and ocean currents.

Most notably for our purposes, the Coriolis force plays a role in coastal upwelling and in wind and weather patterns.

Coastal Upwelling

As the California Current pushes southward along the US West Coast, the top layer of water is deflected a bit to the right (westward) because of the Coriolis effect. The layer under that is deflected slightly more to the west, and so on, with the net result being offshore transport of water along the West Coast. As this water moves offshore, colder, deeper water is drawn upward to replace the water that's moved offshore. This process is called coastal upwelling.

Because this upwelling draws large concentrations of nutrients from deeper water up into the surface zone where sunlight is available, the result is a big boost in productivity across the whole food web. It's recycling on a grand scale, in which the food scraps of the marine environment—dead cells and other organic matter—are composted, transported, and used to fuel new growth at the surface. At the same time, the cross-shore

UPWELLING

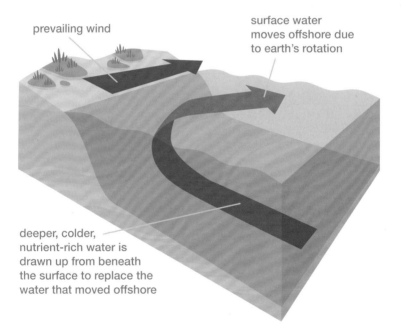

prevailing wind

surface water moves offshore due to earth's rotation

deeper, colder, nutrient-rich water is drawn up from beneath the surface to replace the water that moved offshore

Coastal upwelling happens when surface water moves away from the coast, causing deeper water to move in and take its place. This is largely due to the combination of prevailing winds and the Coriolis effect, most prominently along the western boundaries of continents.

movement of water carries animal larvae and other zooplankton away from shore (during upwelling) or toward shore (as winds relax), influencing when and where animals might settle and grow.

Because coastal upwelling is driven by prevailing winds, it is both seasonal (mostly in summer along the West Coast) and spatially patchy, focused especially on prominent coastal headlands. In the Pacific Northwest, coastal upwelling reaches its peak in June at Cape Blanco, Oregon, the westernmost point in the state.

Wind, Weather, and Climate Patterns

Water deals with heat like a herd of elephants changes directions: it takes an enormous amount of energy to change the temperature of water. The larger the body of water, the more energy is required to change its temperature and, hence, the more stable its temperature. Larger, more stable bodies of water have proportionately more influence on the temperature of everything around them. A small pond, for example, may slightly influence the conditions along its edges—after all, that is one good reason to sit near a pond on a hot summer day. But the Pacific Ocean is a much larger pond, and correspondingly it has a much larger effect: it drives weather and climate at regional and planetary scales.

Being an active continental margin with deep submarine trenches just offshore, the West Coast owes its weather directly to the adjacent vast reservoir of water. As land and air temperatures rise and fall over the course of a day (their temperatures may change by 20 degrees Fahrenheit or more), the Pacific is unmoved, its temperature changing by only a degree or two. In this respect, the Pacific is an ordering force of profound moderation, the steadying bass note to terrestrial tremolo.

The result is predictable winds—onshore in the afternoons, offshore at night—and only moderate differences between seasons along the Pacific Coast. For example, compare Seattle (on the Pacific) with Montreal, Quebec (inland), and Moncton, New Brunswick (on the Atlantic), which all sit at roughly the same latitude. The average high temperature in Seattle—strongly moderated by its proximity to the Pacific—varies from 47 degrees Fahrenheit (in January) to 72 degrees (in July), a 25-degree difference over the year. Montreal, with no ocean nearby, varies more than twice as much between seasons: 24 degrees Fahrenheit (in January) to 80 degrees (in July), a 56-degree difference over the year. And Moncton, on the Atlantic's shallow, passive margin, looks much more like Montreal than Seattle: 26 degrees Fahrenheit (in January) to 78 degrees (in July), a 52-degree difference over the year. The moderating force of deep ocean water is a big part of what creates these differences in temperature between these places.

Coastal fog and upwelling, described above, are also closely tied to the active margin and its associated deep water. And at a local scale, even real-estate prices are affected: there are many reasons coastal real estate is more expensive than real estate elsewhere, but climate is surely one of them. Weather patterns, fog, and sun—not to mention the coastal views that tectonics have ultimately created—are all likely to be wrapped up in the price of a house or apartment.

Waves and Beach Shapes

The energy of prevailing winds creates the waves visible at the beach, although the wave that's breaking right now could be a function of stormy conditions far out at sea days ago. Such wind-driven waves capture energy from the wind and can travel great distances before they encounter shore. As the wave approaches land and the water gets shallower, the wave experiences friction from the sea bottom, slows, and begins to peak. Finally, the wave breaks when the water depth gets shallower than about 5 percent of its wavelength or about 75 percent of the wave's height.

So a wave about one foot high with a wavelength (distance between wave peaks) of about thirty feet will break as it arrives in water about a foot and a half deep. Larger waves will break in deeper water. (If it were otherwise, with very large waves breaking only in very shallow water, surfing would be unreasonably dangerous.)

The depth and shape of the sea bottom therefore influence the shape of the waves. But the converse is also true: the nature of waves shapes the beach; large, powerful waves erode a coastline, while gentler surf may deposit new sediment. Where sandbars tend to move around with tides and currents, the size, shape, and location of waves can change radically over the course of days, as surfers well know. Finally, because of the way that waves bend around solid objects, wave energy tends to converge on rocky headlands and diverge away from sandy beaches nearby.

Generally, the longer the stretch of uninterrupted water for winds to blow across—a measure known as fetch—the larger the swells. This is why the central Oregon coast experiences much larger waves than, say, Friday Harbor, Washington. Central Oregon faces the open expanse of the Pacific, while Friday Harbor sits on the lee side of an island in a well-protected cove—which is precisely why it is a good harbor.

Waves also influence both the beach slope and the size of sand grains that make up the beach. Finer-grained beaches tend to be flatter, because both swash (movement of water up the beach after a wave breaks) and the backwash (as the surf recedes back to the ocean following a wave breaking) have about the same amount of energy, distributing the grains evenly across the beach. On beaches consisting of coarse sand or pebbles, where grain size is large, the swash carries grains up the beach, but wave energy is lost as the water flows among grains, and so the backwash is proportionately weaker. The result is a steeper beach.

Compare, for example, two beaches in Oregon. Threemile Beach (near Coos Bay) is 40 percent steeper than Whiskey Run (near Bandon). Threemile accordingly has sand grains about 25 percent larger. This physical effect trickles down to ecology, as well: in part because of the steeper slope and larger grains, Threemile hosts about 25 percent fewer species than Whiskey Run.

El Niño and the Pacific Decadal Oscillation

Because environmental conditions along the West Coast depend so strongly on the Pacific Ocean, relatively small changes in ocean conditions can mean large consequences for coastal systems. Some such changes constitute unpredictable year-to-year variation, but some of the most important shifts in ocean conditions are recurring. Over the past decades, scientists have described multiple large-scale climate oscillations in the Pacific. Two of these are prominent and help us understand year-to-year variability in ocean conditions.

El Niño (or more properly, the El Niño–Southern Oscillation, ENSO) is perhaps the better known of these, driven by a weakening of winds and a warming of surface waters in the eastern tropical Pacific. This leads to an array of changes around the Pacific, including warmer waters along the US West Coast, weaker winds and upwelling, and reduced productivity along the coasts of Washington, Oregon, and California. The ecological effects are visible and widespread, including poor fisheries catches, declines in kelp abundance, and decreased pupping success in marine mammals. El Niño events occur at approximately three- to seven-year intervals, and some events are much stronger than others. Interestingly, conditions tend to return to a normal or neutral phase when El Niño subsides. A third phase of the oscillation is known as La Niña, which brings periods of cooler-than-average water temperatures and strong winter storms to the Pacific Northwest.

The Pacific Decadal Oscillation (PDO), admittedly a less imaginative name, operates over decades rather than years, alternating between "warm" and "cool" phases in the North Pacific. These phases can last a decade or more. The mechanism behind these oscillations is linked to large-scale changes in patterns of sea-surface temperature and sea-level pressure in the North Pacific. The effect of PDO phase is dramatic; those few degrees of change in sea-surface temperature can mean the difference between good and bad decades for salmon productivity. For example, cool phases of the PDO are good for salmon returns to the rivers of Washington and Oregon. The effects of the PDO extend to terrestrial ecosystems too. In some cases, the phase of the PDO can be detected in the rings of oak trees miles from the coast, illustrating the importance of ocean temperature and offering a useful tool for reconstructing historical climate cycles.

GEOLOGY AS DESTINY: EVERYDAY EFFECTS FOR THE SHORELINE VISITOR

At the most basic level, life along an active tectonic margin means more rocky shoreline habitat, resulting in more habitat for crabs and snails and kelp and other hard-substrate species, and less habitat for clams and sand dollars and other soft-substrate dwellers. The deep water just offshore can moderate temperature swings over the course of a day or a year, and they cause fairly predictable winds that switch daily between onshore and off-shore directions (see p. 47). Fog often follows, to the benefit of land plants in the coastal zone. Upwelling causes an increase in primary productivity, which in turn fuels larger, more diverse suites of species living in these areas and, consequently, more complex food webs.

The ecological effects of these factors are dramatic. For example, the West Coast has about a hundred different species of chitons, while along most of the passive coastal margin of the East Coast, there is only one. Similarly, kelps, limpets, and other rocky habitat groups exhibit greater diversity along the West Coast than the East Coast. This diversity can be traced to the geological history of the region combined with high biological productivity and high habitat complexity. Over long periods of time, these processes have created the diversity we see on the shores of Washington and Oregon.

A beachcast kelp remains firmly attached to its cobble anchor

Sandy beaches in Washington tend to be broad and flat.

Second Beach, bookended by rocky headlands

LIVING
BETWEEN
THE TIDES

W hat lives where, and why? It's a complicated question with many answers, and this is what keeps ecologists interested in their jobs. Layered on top of earth-history factors (chapter 1), real-time pressures are constantly shaping life along the shore.

Where members of a species live in a particular place, we can assume that the conditions there are favorable for survival: food is available, water and air temperatures are tolerable, and so on. Other members of its species are probably also there, and so are its predators.

And what is an ecosystem, exactly? It's the sum of interactions among the elements at a given time and place, both living (animals and plants) and nonliving (sunlight and rocks and water). The term therefore grows and shrinks to encompass an area of interest or a place to study, et cetera. A sandy beach can be an ecosystem, as can an estuary or mudflat. At larger scales, the entire West Coast with all its varied habitats is often considered a single ecosystem.

More than simply being a handy term for a set of places and things, the word *ecosystem* also has a deeper sense that suggests the importance of interactions. By analogy, just as the global economy is a product of billions of market interactions among people with diverse goals, ecosystems are a product of a multitude of interactions among organisms and the environment. And just as the economy can behave in unexpected and sometimes dramatic ways, ecosystems can do the same, for the same reasons: both economies and ecosystems are precarious, ever-changing arrangements, with many forces acting upon and shaping them. Both have an inherent capacity to surprise.

Given its complexity, shoreline ecology might seem driven by pure happenstance. But a closer look, underpinned by decades of study by thousands of people, has revealed some of the important patterns and processes governing what lives where. In short, there are rules by which nature plays. Or perhaps *guidelines* better describes the mix of predictable outcomes and chance that seems to structure life along the shore.

The mix of species at a shoreline site in Washington or Oregon differs from its counterpart in Santa Barbara, California, because of differences in climate and oceanography and history, but also because of the other species found nearby. The idea that creatures living in a place can determine what other creatures can live in that place is one of the core insights of ecology, but it also seems a bit circular. It means that the order in which species arrive in an ecosystem matters, and it also underscores how tightly interconnected each species is within an ecosystem.

NONLIVING ELEMENTS THAT SHAPE ECOSYSTEMS

Tides, temperature and sunlight are three of the dominant physical forces in intertidal areas, and they interact in complicated ways to influence where plants and animals live on the shore. Though it is difficult to separate the effects of these forces, it is important nonetheless to understand the general influence of each and their outsize role in shaping ecosystems.

Tides

The rise and fall of the tides creates a habitat like no other on earth. Over a period of several hours, land becomes sea, sea becomes land, and species living between the two experience a wholesale change of surroundings. Eons of tidal oscillations have shaped a vibrant and diverse set of species that exist nowhere else but this intertidal zone.

Essentially, tides are very large waves that slosh around ocean basins; the local crest of such waves creates high tide and the trough creates low tide. Gravity drives these large waves as the sun and moon pull on the ocean's water. The highest high tides and lowest low tides occur when the

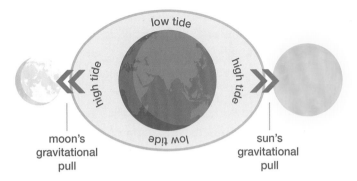

Tides are very large waves created by the gravitational effects of both the sun and the moon. When the sun and moon line up, the magnitude of the tide is at its maximum.

sun and moon are pulling in the same direction—that is, every two weeks, when the moon is full and again when the moon is new.

These semimonthly periods of very high and very low tides are often referred to as spring tides, but don't be fooled: they are unrelated to the season that we call spring; rather, these are periods when the tide "springs forth." Between these periods of spring tide, the moon and sun are pulling at angles to each other, reducing the magnitude of the tides. These periods of more moderate tides are known as neap tides.

The US West Coast and many other places on earth experience two unequal high tides and two unequal low tides each day. Some places in the world have only a single high and low tide each day, due to the placement of continents, and some have only negligible tidal variation.

On the West Coast, the waves that create tides propagate northward along the shore, causing high or low tide to be earlier in the day in Oregon than in Washington. As a general rule, the farther north we go, the bigger the difference between high and low tide, with the result that tides in Alaska are more extreme than tides in California. In Puget Sound, the difference between the highest and lowest tides of the day can be ten vertical feet or more, which can translate to hundreds of horizontal feet of intertidal habitat.

Time and Tide and Temperature

Species that live between the high- and low-tide lines are tightly tuned to the tides. Some feed at high tide, hiding the rest of the day. Others do the opposite. All must deal with dramatic swings in temperature associated with changing tides: as the tide ebbs, intertidal temperatures increase in summer (and may decrease in winter) as once-submerged land is exposed to the air.

Cold water can sap heat from a warm intertidal zone almost instantly as the tide returns on a summer day, creating a kind of temperature whiplash for resident species. Imagine plunging from a warm sundeck into a cold ocean. Then imagine staying in that cold ocean for six hours until the tide turns again, after which you are left high and dry. Then imagine repeating this sequence every six hours for your entire life.

Warmer temperatures during daylight hours tend to boost metabolism and accelerate growth, to a point. But a hot sun and warm air temperatures during a low tide can quickly cause significant stress and even mortality. While some intertidal seaweeds such as those in the genus *Pyropia*—often eaten as nori—easily tolerate desiccation, drying and overheating can kill many other species within minutes to hours. As a consequence, daytime low tides during the summer have a profound influence on who lives where along the coast: only those that can tolerate these extreme swings in conditions will survive long. Nighttime low tides, too, can be dangerous, since in northern regions, extreme low tides occur at night in winter. Nighttime low tides that coincide with unusual cold spells can be cold enough to freeze organisms or even whole tidepools.

MICROCLIMATES

Overlaid on the temperature effects associated with tidal cycles is the familiar association between temperature and latitude: as a general rule, air, land, and sea temperatures all become cooler as we move northward toward the pole. This is why San Diego, California, draws more beachgoers than does Seattle.

But local factors cause both air and water temperature to vary along the coast, creating a mosaic of habitats that does not follow a strict pattern.

We might find cooler water temperatures in southern Oregon than along the Washington coast, for instance; at smaller scales, a deep bay may be cooler than an adjacent shallow bay.

And at even smaller scales, we could find cooler temperatures under an overhang or in a shaded place compared with a neighboring area exposed to full sun. For example, shaded surfaces can be 20 degrees Fahrenheit cooler than unshaded surfaces nearby, and as a consequence, a snail sitting in direct sunlight might have more than twice the metabolic rate of its shaded neighbor. Correspondingly, we find differences in the organisms occupying these areas that reflect these temperature conditions.

PHYSICAL EFFECTS OF TEMPERATURE

Temperature isn't just a feeling; it acts at a molecular level, too, influencing many of the processes that make life possible. This includes everything from photosynthesis through metabolism, and even the firing of neurons that is necessary for every perception and every movement.

Examples abound to illustrate how finely tuned these mechanisms can be, but two will suffice: there's an Antarctic fish whose eye proteins start to deform as water warms just a degree or two, and that same temperature span of just a degree or two can be the difference, in humans, between having a fever and being dead.

The point is that each species has a range of body temperatures within which their chemistry works well, and different species have different ranges. Because we find different air and water temperatures along the coast, we expect to find different communities of species in different places.

Sunlight

Sunlight obviously warms up the intertidal. But sunlight does much more than that: it is an essential component for most of the life on earth. Daytime brings the energy needed for photosynthesis, through which algae and plants, in a feat of chemical engineering, convert sunlight and air into sugar and water. The sugars become the food that fuels the nearshore food web. The waste product is oxygen; indeed, the vast majority of oxygen in the air is the by-product of photosynthesis, and about half the oxygen we breathe comes from photosynthesis in the ocean. If you take two breaths to let this fact sink in, you can thank ocean photosynthesizers for one of those breaths.

The colorful pigments characteristic of seaweeds and seagrasses play an essential role in this process. The patchwork of colors splashed across the intertidal zone, from gold and brown to green, red, and even pink, is an indication of the photosynthetic machinery at work in this system.

Salinity

Ocean salinity is nearly constant worldwide: 3.5 percent, commonly expressed as thirty-five parts per thousand. If you've ever tried to drink seawater, you have some appreciation for the vast practical difference that 3.5 percent makes. Apart from making seawater nowhere close to drinkable for humans, salinity changes the fundamental qualities of water. Salt water is denser than freshwater by 2 to 3 percent and conducts electricity thousands of times better. And seawater has more *stuff* dissolved in it than freshwater.

That dissolved stuff is known as solute. To kelp, fish, and many other ocean organisms, it's what keeps the concentration of water in their cells balanced with the surrounding salt water. Put a kelp frond in freshwater, and this balance is immediately thrown off; water will rush into the kelp's cells, which will consequently swell and may burst. If you've ever walked on the beach after a rainstorm, you may have seen beach-cast kelps that are unusually lumpy: this is the effect of freshwater on kelp tissues. The same thing happens to your fingers if you've been in a bath too long.

Most species are adapted to either freshwater or salt water, and that's why we think of marine and freshwater species as belonging to different communities. But right along the shore, where salinity tends to be lower and more variable than in the open ocean, many species tolerate a substantial change in salinity. Estuaries, for example, require such flexibility, and it is also helpful for species living in tidepools (where salinity can climb high during periods of evaporation) and for those that move between saltwater and freshwater habitats.

Salmon are probably the best-known example of such a lifestyle; they hatch in freshwater, spend one or more years in the ocean, and then return to freshwater to reproduce. Salmon switch worlds in this way using molecular pumps to move excess salt out of their cells while in salt water.

Most species, however, prefer a relatively narrow range of salinities, and conditions can get stressful when local conditions change the salinity. Freshwater from rivers and melting glaciers can substantially dilute seawater and, conversely, evaporation can increase salinity in shallow areas—the Dead Sea is the most famous example, and it is dead for precisely this reason.

In estuaries or where streams and rivers reach the shore, denser seawater often floats on top of salt water, forming a freshwater "lens" that can be inches or feet thick. During a rainstorm in the Salish Sea, for example, it is possible to stand with your feet in salt water and to drink water that's nearly fresh off the seawater's surface at knee level (although we would not recommend this practice). The freshwater doesn't float for long—over a period of hours or days, it mixes with the saltier water through the action of tides, currents, and winds.

Energy

What powers an ecosystem? What makes it go?

In the realm of biology, we most often think of chemical energy as the currency of living things, with which cells make sugars, proteins, and lipids to carry out the day-to-day functions of being alive. When one individual eats another, stored energy is transferred from the eaten to the eater, although this process is notoriously inefficient, and something like 90 percent of energy can be lost as waste and heat between one link in the food chain and the next. Even so, the food web is a sort of wiring diagram for an ecological community, illustrating where chemical energy comes from and where it goes.

Perhaps a more familiar form of energy is kinetic energy, which is the kind associated with motion. Kinetic energy comes visibly into play along the shore. Just as you might use a whisk to beat air into a bowl of cream to make whipped cream, waves along the shore beat air into the surface layers of the ocean, creating bubbles and in the process help-ing to dissolve oxygen and carbon dioxide into the water. For animals breathing oxygen directly from the water—and nearly all animals in the ocean do this—dissolved oxygen is a critical measure of who can live where. For plants and other organisms that take up carbon dioxide, the concentration of CO_2 has the same importance. Waves mix things up, continually refreshing surface waters, keeping ocean and atmosphere tightly connected.

In back bays and lazy estuaries, the lack of wave energy leads directly to a lack of chemical energy and generally to a lower diversity of species living in those places. Slow water movement can reduce the exchange of nutrients among coastal areas and increase the accumulation of fine particulate matter, creating muddy habitats. Where water flow is very low or static, black mud can form. This mud can be entirely devoid of dissolved oxygen, a condition referred to as anoxia. The color and atten-dant sulfurous smell result from specialized bacteria having moved in to take advantage of the low-oxygen condition. The really objectionable smell is due to hydrogen sulfide gas, produced as microbes decompose organic matter in the absence of oxygen. Other than these bacteria, not much lives in anoxic mud. Hydrogen sulfide production is typical in anaerobic sediments (those that lack oxygen) that form a layer beneath the more oxygenated surface sediments. When the sediments in black mud are churned up, hydrogen sulfide is released.

When ecologists refer to high-energy or low-energy environments, kinetic energy is generally what springs to mind: a coast being pounded by waves clearly has a lot of kinetic energy. But because these waves mix air and nutrients in the surface layer of the ocean, places with high kinetic energy are very often places with high productivity and correspondingly high chemical energy. And as a result, high-energy environments often support a more diverse suite of species than low-energy environments. Interestingly, humans seem almost universally to find high-energy envi-ronments more aesthetically attractive; surely computer desktop images of wave-swept shores outnumber those of mudflats by a large margin worldwide.

An example of a high-energy environment, near Depoe Bay, Oregon

Wave Action, Exposure, and Disturbance

Wave action is a defining characteristic of any coastal site. Waves can be generated by local winds, or they can arise from distant weather systems that are unaffected by local conditions.

Scientists often describe particular sites as more or less exposed, which is shorthand for the degree of wave action and kinetic energy we expect there; more-exposed sites are subject to larger and more frequent waves, while less-exposed sites tend to be protected from wave forces. More-exposed sites typically have a long fetch (the length of water over which the wind has blown before reaching the site): envision a beach with an uninterrupted view of the horizon. Less-exposed sites have shorter fetch lengths, occurring, for example, in bays, in coves, or behind islands or headlands. Wave exposure indicates how much wave force an organism experiences in a particular place.

The energy that comes with wave exposure is a major underlying force that shapes communities along the shore. Some species tolerate battering by waves by being very stiff (e.g., mussels); others are quite flexible (e.g., feather boa kelp, *Egregia menziesii*); still others adopt a streamlined shape (e.g., limpets). Some grow in clumps or clusters that help to shed wave forces. Some seaweeds bend with the waves and have elastic structures that snap back into place once the wave energy has dissipated. Many animals, in addition to having streamlined forms, adapt their behaviors to resist the waves: limpets, chitons, abalone, and others tend to clamp down hard on the rocks or other firm surfaces, resisting the pressures to be dislodged.

Those species that can't tolerate wave forces require calmer conditions, where they maintain their space by being superior competitors or predators. Consequently, a visitor might find one species abundant on a headland, only to find that it disappears around the corner where conditions are more protected. For example, kelp species that occupy the most-exposed locations on rocky headlands typically aren't found in less-exposed areas nearby. Likewise, kelp species that favor calmer conditions aren't found in the most-exposed locations. The result is a gradient of species along the shore that is shaped by physical forces.

Waves can also rearrange intertidal communities, either on their own due to the sheer momentum of the water or, in some cases, by shifting boulders and logs, crushing unlucky seaweeds and invertebrates. Storms that create larger-than-normal waves expose plants and animals living along the shore to conditions that are rougher than usual, often killing some fraction of the organisms on shore.

But the losses created by such disturbances are tempered by eventual gains: patches of space opened by disturbances create opportunities for other seaweeds and invertebrates to move in, opening new real estate in an otherwise crowded neighborhood. Disturbance can therefore be a source of renewal in intertidal communities, and it is often seasonal: waves on the outer coast of Washington dislodge a given patch of mussels on average every seven or eight years, and strong winter storms are ten times more likely to have this effect than waves during the rest of the year.

The sea palm (*Postelsia palmaeformis*) is a great example of a disturbance-dependent species. It lives exclusively on wave-swept rocks in the most-exposed environments along the West Coast. It *could* live

The sea palm (*Postelsia palmaeformis*) grows among mussels and barnacles on wave-swept shores.

in other places, except that mussels outcompete the sea palm for space, so mussels generally dominate and suppress the sea palm before it gets a chance to grow. In very wave-exposed environments, however, waves clear patches of mussels, opening space for this kelp to move in. Sea palms tend to grow in clumps consisting of many individuals: this configuration, along with their flexible stipes (stalks), helps them shed wave forces and persist in the most wave-swept locations.

Nutrients, Oxygen, and Carbon Dioxide

Basic life processes require just a handful of ingredients. For primary producers—plants, algae, and their allies—life needs only sunlight, a source of carbon dioxide (CO_2) or a related compound, water, and a few nutrients (the main ones being nitrogen and phosphorus).

In air, CO_2 is generally not the factor that limits plant growth. So, for example, in caring for a houseplant or a garden, ensuring that the garden has sufficient sunlight, nutrients (nitrogen, phosphorus, and perhaps potassium), and water is usually sufficient. The creation of plant material, or plant biomass, is often referred to as primary production, and it is generally followed by secondary production as snails and bugs and other things (including you and your family) that eat the new plants increase in biomass. It's easy to imagine that the success of a garden depends at least in part on the availability of raw materials to create biomass.

It works the same way in the ocean, where primary production depends on the availability of sunlight, nutrients, and CO_2. By and large, the surface ocean has plenty of sunlight and CO_2, so the factor that limits primary production is often the availability of nutrients such as nitrogen and phosphorus. These two nutrients plus others are supplied to the ocean in runoff from land or via deposition from the air. Once in the ocean, nutrients are transported by water motion or moved around by animals as they excrete waste materials or eventually die and decompose. As nutrients sink out of the surface layers, they can be transported back toward the surface by coastal upwelling. Such mechanisms fertilize the intertidal garden, which in turn supports the diversity of life dependent on this primary production.

Animals, by contrast, don't directly harvest their own energy from the sun. So animals often eat those species that do, just as garden snails eat growing vegetables.

But in addition to food, animals need oxygen to survive and grow. Humans and other land animals, of course, get our oxygen from the air, and many marine animals can do the same, at least for limited periods of time—for example, you can chase a lobster around your kitchen if you are so inclined.

With the important exception of marine mammals, animals that spend much or all of their lives underwater need some way of getting oxygen while submerged. They do so by using gills or similar structures to remove oxygen that is dissolved in the water. But there's a catch: dissolved oxygen is in relatively short supply in seawater. So the churning that happens along the coast in the form of wave action makes a big difference, mixing air into the water and helping to dissolve oxygen. Photosynthesis can add oxygen to seawater too, just as keeping houseplants may increase the oxygen indoors.

In sum, anywhere there is sunlight and a sufficient supply of nutrients, algae are likely to thrive. Where algae and other primary producers are in abundance, the rest of the food web often follows suit, particularly where ample oxygen and kinetic energy are found, building complexity and biomass on a base of small photosynthesizers.

Wind

Wind is a persistent force along the West Coast, a fact of life. Wind is the movement of air from one place to another.

Onshore winds, also known as sea breezes or day breezes, are locally generated winds blowing onto shore from the ocean. They tend to be a daily feature, developing in the afternoon along the West Coast as air rushes from relatively cool high-pressure areas over water to warmer low-pressure areas over land—hence, San Francisco's afternoon fog during the summer. The pattern relaxes as land cools overnight, resulting in the opposite pattern in the morning, with air moving from land to ocean. These morning offshore winds, or land breezes, are favored by surfers because they produce waves that hold their shape.

Prevailing winds are those that tend to blow consistently in one direction. They are caused by larger-scale patterns of movement in the earth's atmosphere. Along the West Coast, prevailing winds tend to blow from the northwest. Prevailing winds generate waves and cause coastal upwelling.

The ecological effects of wind, whatever its source, are perhaps not obvious, but they are important. Intertidal organisms must find ways to deal with wind and its effects. For example, as wind passes over a plant or animal, it leads to a certain degree of evaporation, drawing water out of the plant or animal and into the air. As the moisture goes from liquid form (in the body) to gaseous form (in the air), the plant or animal cools off in the process. More succinctly: drying is cooling.

Many species—for example, mussels, barnacles, and seaweeds—cannot move away from harsh conditions. Instead, they have developed traits that allow them to cope with desiccation (drying) and heat. Mussels, barnacles, limpets, and others are capable of tightly closing their shells

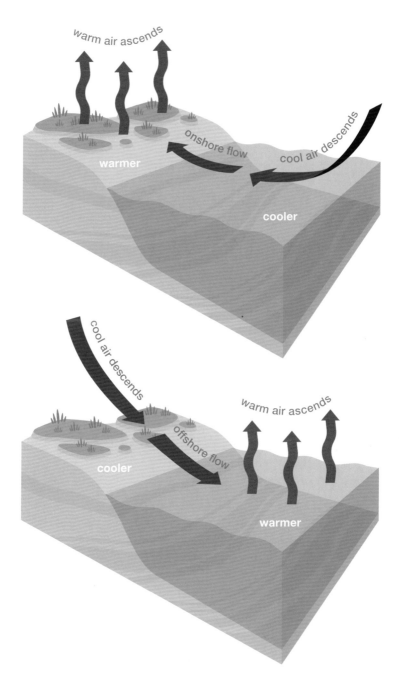

Coastal wind patterns shift between onshore flow during the afternoon (top) and offshore flow in the morning (bottom).

Many seaweeds that live in intertidal areas, like this rockweed (*Fucus distichus*), can tolerate drying and then rehydrate quickly when the tide returns.

to preserve interior moisture, sealing themselves off from the drying surroundings; other species cluster together to reduce their combined exposed surface area—for instance, a large patch of anemones heats and dries far slower than does a single anemone.

These and other animals often slow their metabolisms during stressful periods, reducing both energy requirements and the accumulation of waste products that are difficult to purge from a tightly closed shell. Some seaweeds, on the other hand, have adopted the opposite strategy for dealing with heat and drying: they simply dry out and live to tell about it. Many intertidal seaweeds can lose a remarkable amount of water without lasting damage, then rehydrate when the tide rises again.

LIVING ELEMENTS THAT SHAPE ECOSYSTEMS

Returning to our overarching question—what lives where, and why?—it's clear that physical forces like sun, wind, and tides play a big role. But the neighbors matter a lot too. The other species living nearby can mean the difference between a site being habitable and uninhabitable.

Neighbors might be helpful. For example, seaweeds can provide cover for small animals, reducing their exposure to sun and wind and predators, and their blades can provide surfaces to live on. But neighboring seaweeds and invertebrates often compete for resources including space and food. Space especially can be limiting in the intertidal, just as it is in dense urban areas where humans compete for housing. And neighbors can be predators too, preferring to eat nearby residents rather than simply steal their space.

A century of ecological research has endeavored to distill the messy, complicated interactions among living things into the kinds of solid,

LARVAL DEVELOPMENT AND TRANSPORT

Seaweeds, mussels, barnacles, tube worms, oysters, anemones, sponges, tunicates . . . many of the most obvious species in the intertidal zone are literally stuck in place. Indeed, many make their own glue or cement, banking on its strength to keep them anchored in spite of the oncoming waves. And even those that aren't permanently place-bound are unlikely to transport themselves over any serious distance: it is difficult to imagine a sea star, snail, or hermit crab moving from one rocky outcrop to the next, let alone across state lines. And yet these species cover our shores. How did they get there?

Most species at the shore have a life history quite different than our own. They typically start out as microscopic larvae, passing through one or more (or twelve) larval stages before reaching a recognizable form in adulthood. Just as a butterfly begins life as a caterpillar, a barnacle is first a nauplius, a clam is first a veliger, and an urchin is first a pluteus. If you are a person who enjoys extremely specific, arcane vocabulary, larval biology might be the field for you.

Seaweeds are far stranger and more complex than most animals in this regard. Rather than having mere larval stages, many seaweeds can pass through unrecognizably different growth forms—microscopic spores and gametes, and larger forms that are crustose, upright, or bladed—that have differing numbers of chromosomes along the way. For example, *Mastocarpus* is a genus of seaweed (see Tar Spot Algae in chapter 6, The Southern Oregon Coast) that has two life stages that are so different that one form was originally described as an entirely different genus.

For many intertidal species, the larval, spore, or gamete phase is the chance to disperse, free of the constraints of the adult form, swimming or otherwise being transported away from parents, possibly to colonize new territory. This behavior makes marine invertebrates and seaweed species similar to wind-dispersed land plants: essentially stuck in one place as adults, depending on currents, wind, and water to leapfrog offspring toward parts unknown. And as in land plants, the success rate of marine invertebrates and seaweeds is likely to be very low. Generally, marine species make many thousands (or hundreds of thousands) of microscopic propagules for every single one that survives to reproduce. A few drops of seawater may contain larvae from many species, a soup of marine miniatures; if you've ever accidentally swallowed seawater, you've quite possibly swallowed snails, worms, sea stars, oysters, and other animals all in the same mouthful.

Larval behavior explains in part why empty space is at a premium in the intertidal: given that billions of larvae float by at any one time, chances are good that at least one will settle out and sit on any given hard surface. Hence, barnacles have forever been the bane of the existence of both sailors and whales.

comforting rules that govern the physical world. When we drop an apple, that apple predictably falls and hits the ground with a known force. But there are no such bright-line rules to predict, say, what happens when we add a new species of snail to an existing tidepool community or precisely what might result when a storm bashes the coastline with massive cedar logs, killing existing species along a shoreline and opening up space for new recruits.

The many interactions among many living species seem to preclude the kind of falling-apple physics rules that ecologists envy, but a few categories of interactions help to simplify ecological dynamics. Among these are competition, predation, and facilitation. Recognizing these categories in the field helps the observer understand what's happening at a site and make good guesses about what will happen next. And it can help to be able to recognize and name the players, either by their common or scientific names, which offers challenges of its own.

Competition: Striving for Real Estate and Food

Competition is largely what it sounds like. Imagine two siblings given a cookie to share. Both will almost certainly compete to maximize their share of a common resource (the cookie), each spending time and energy to ward off the other, ultimately ending up with less cookie than either would have in the absence of the sibling.

Ecological competition can be less direct than this and can happen between individuals of different species, but the idea is the same: everyone loses a bit, and some (often the smaller competitors) lose big. The same dynamic plays out on every rock or patch of sand along the shore, with each individual of each species struggling to maximize its share of common resources, be they food, space, sunlight, or other necessities.

Along the shore, competition for space can be particularly intense, given the narrow sliver of real estate between land and sea. Seawater is teeming with the spores of algae and with larvae and juveniles of all sorts of animals. Under the right conditions, these early life stages will settle down and grow into adult forms. A primary necessity for settlement is space to land on. Consequently, bare space tends not to stay unoccupied

Space to settle and grow in rocky intertidal habitats can be scarce, and organisms often are densely packed. Here, a single mussel is surrounded by a host of gooseneck barnacles, its shell providing substrate for tiny barnacles and a couple of limpets.

for long, and where bare space is limiting, species often grow right on top of another. Photosynthesizers need sun, others need food and shelter from pounding waves and baking sun, and so every species has to deal with constant competition for space that meets its needs. Some species—for example, sea stars and limpets—clear space on hard surfaces, allowing other animals and seaweeds to move in. Other disturbances, like a log bashing against the rocks in high surf, can similarly open space.

Those lucky enough to find an open spot on the rocks, and whose neighbors don't crowd them out, might persist for many years. Food for these animals, such as barnacles and mussels, is plankton, delivered by moving water, and is generally not something they need to worry about in productive temperate waters. Grazing invertebrates, too, such as small crustaceans, limpets, snails, chitons, and others often have plenty of food available, since algae can be found year-round. Competition for food is a larger factor for predators, as in seabirds competing for small fish and those same fish competing for invertebrates.

Some species do best when they settle among members of the same species; often, groups tolerate drying and wave stress better than individuals do on their own, and living in groups means there's always a chance to mate. This logic applies to mussels, acorn and gooseneck barnacles, anemones, limpets, and many others. And many clever invertebrates

INVASIVE SPECIES

Invasive (or introduced or exotic or nonnative) species are often described in vaguely threatening terms. Famous examples in the US include everything from the zebra mussels of the Great Lakes to eucalyptus trees to the common earthworm. Each of these species evolved and developed elsewhere, and humans brought each to the US, where they found ready habitat and thrived. There are thousands of examples across every habitat you can name, including the seashore.

But in a Darwinian world with nature red in tooth and claw, why should we care? Aren't humans merely accelerating movements of species around the globe, and shouldn't the fittest species win out? Isn't that the way of the world?

Popular on seafood menus, the Manila clam (*Venerupis philippinarum*) is native to Asian waters but has taken up residence throughout Puget Sound.

As an ethical matter, we must be concerned with the degree of harm humans cause by introducing species from one place to another. Each species is the unique product of millions of years of evolution; when human-introduced species cause extinctions of local flora and fauna, we lose these lifeforms forever. From this perspective, introduced species are simply another way in which humans cause the loss of lineages millions of years old. Moreover, we (humans) are conscious of our actions and—depending on one's ethical framework—we have an obligation to minimize harm to our planet for the benefit of present and future generations.

At a practical level, billions of dollars and untold labor in mitigating invasive species, and the consequences of radically altered habitats, all argue against the wisdom of continuing to introduce species from around the globe.

Nonnative species continue to dramatically reshape our shores. For example, two such imported shoreline creatures—the purple varnish clam (*Nuttalia obscurata*), introduced in the 1990s, and the Asian mud snail (*Batillaria attramentaria*), introduced in the 1920s—so dominate some beaches that visitors might find it impossible to imagine the beach without them. The pair change the very nature of the sandy beach, leaving little open space at the surface and riddling the subsurface with holes.

Both species occur in Washington and Oregon, along with other nonnative predators like the Japanese oyster drill (*Ocinebrellus inornatus*) and the European green crab (*Carcinus maenas*), but are more common in the protected waters of the Salish Sea than on the outer coast. And this is a general trend: more sheltered waters seem to have more invasive species, whether they are brought for commerce (e.g., the Pacific oyster, *Crassostrea gigas*) or merely are by-products of international commerce (e.g., *Sargassum* spp. and *Zostera japonica*—see Estuaries in chapter 5, The Northern Oregon Coast). Much of the biota on rocky shorelines in Washington and Oregon is still mainly native species.

and seaweeds use chemical cues to lead them to favorable places to settle, ensuring they grow up near a suitable source of food, mates, or substrate.

If there's a patch of bare rock between the tides, look around for the explanation. There may be some limpets nearby, which mow down algae and use their wedge-like shells to dislodge animals such as barnacles, or even other limpets, from the rock. Or there might be piles of driftwood on the beach above the high-tide line, the vast majority of which arrived by sea. Waves might have driven those logs onto the rocks, clearing space—a physical, rather than biological, explanation for the bare rock.

Predation: Eating One Another

Then there is the fact that intertidal neighbors are hungry and could choose to eat one another. Marine animals have evolved an impressive array of ways to consume each other. Most obviously, large predators such as sharks and marine mammals can tear prey into pieces using a mouthful of teeth. This is likely the image that springs to mind as the first example of a predator in the ocean, and indeed these kinds of high-profile species are routinely found along the West Coast (although, thankfully, not typically in intertidal areas).

But to biologists, predation is a far broader idea: it occurs any time one living thing eats another, regardless of whether the prey happens to be an animal, plant, or anything else alive. (For example, you picking and eating berries qualifies as predation.)

Predation can be challenging to see among some of the smaller organisms on the shore; we have to look pretty closely to see the action as they endeavor to eat without being eaten. And while we often think of predators as pursuing their prey, many acts of predation at the shore are carried out by organisms fixed in place. All those barnacles and mussels and anemones need to eat too.

SO MANY WAYS OF EATING

For example, barnacles cement themselves to the rock, essentially landing on their heads as larvae and then building their shells around them directly on the hard surface. From there, they use modified legs that look like feathers to reach into the water and pull out tiny bits of suspended food that include plankton and detritus. This is called suspension feeding, and it is used in various forms by many intertidal invertebrates.

Clams, oysters, mussels, and the like also feed by capturing small particles. They do this by extending a siphon, complete with incurrent and excurrent capabilities, to draw in water, filtering out the food particles and spitting out the remaining water. This is known as filter feeding.

A wide variety of animals from worms to sea cucumbers filter sediment, rather than water, looking for food and leaving behind a trail of discarded sediment. Deposit feeding (as this is known) is a lifestyle that works on land too: it has followed our earthworms out of the sea and into our fields.

Anemones use a far different strategy to capture prey. With their bodies fixed on the substrate, they spread their tentacles and lie in wait for potential prey to make contact. The tentacles contain specialized stinging cells that are used to immobilize small prey. Once immobilized, the tentacles move the prey to the mouth, where it is eaten.

Some anemones hedge their nutritional bets by also maintaining single-celled algae in their outer layers. These algae contain light-harvesting pigments and carry out photosynthesis while living within the host animal. The anemone benefits from its houseguests, collecting some of the compounds the algae produce via photosynthesis. The anemones' relatives, the tropical reef-building corals, employ the same strategy.

Invertebrates that can move around have developed different means of feeding. Snails and their allies use specialized feeding structures called radulae (hundreds of teeth arranged on what looks like a tiny belt sander)—to scrape algae from rocks or bore into the shells of their prey. And for good measure, some limpets and chitons cover their radulae with iron, creating rows of metal teeth.

Urchins, on the other hand, have evolved a radically different design for rasping. They use radially symmetrical fivefold teeth to graze kelp and other fleshy seaweeds. Urchins can consume so much seaweed that they create entire zones that are barren of fleshy seaweeds. Sand dollars have mouthparts similar to those of urchins, but instead of using their teeth to

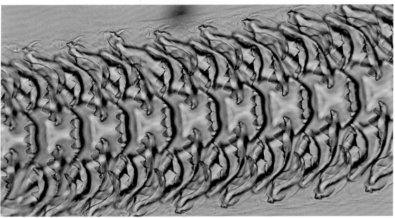

Anemones (top) ensnare passing food particles with their tentacles. Some snails can change the shape of their teeth in their radulae (feeding organs; bottom) depending on their food source. Bottom photo by Sasha Seroy.

feed, they use hydraulic tube feet to collect zooplankton and other small particles from seawater. Sea stars famously evert their stomachs to digest prey outside of their bodies, while their relatives the sea cucumbers use tentacles to ingest detritus.

A sea star wraps around a lone mussel in an effort to eat the soft tissues inside.

Intertidal crabs use prominent claws to crush the shells of their prey and complicated mouthparts to slice and tear the prey into manageable bits. Fish also feed in the intertidal, many with jaws quite similar to our own. And when the tide is out, land mammals often bring their own jaws into the intertidal: raccoons, otters, deer, and even bears frequently eat invertebrates or seaweed along the shore.

The above examples are by no means exhaustive. Several hundred million years of evolution has produced a kaleidoscope of predatory strategies among animal lineages, surely many of which we have not yet even discovered.

OFFENSE AND DEFENSE

The dual needs to eat and to avoid being eaten have shaped evolution in the sea for at least 550 million years. The result has been an arms race of sorts, with those having slightly stronger shells or claws or teeth surviving to pass their traits along to their offspring, while their prey respond by developing stronger defense mechanisms over time. The fossil record shows animals evolving successive waves of offensive and defensive traits, and today's species are only the most recent products of this long process.

Shells, jaws, and other hard parts in marine creatures are made from compounds found in seawater. Most commonly, these parts are calcium carbonate—familiar as classroom chalk, which is itself formed by the accumulation of tiny shells of marine creatures. Calcium carbonate is readily formed from seawater, and hence it is both ubiquitous and critically important for both predation and defense to predation. Other hard parts, such as the intricate pillbox-shaped shells of microscopic diatoms that fill the sunlit ocean, form from silicon dioxide, most familiar to us as glass.

Plants and seaweeds too have evolved mechanisms to deter grazing. Similar to invertebrates, some seaweeds deposit calcium carbonate in their cell walls to protect their tissues from grazers. Other seaweeds have developed elaborate chemical defenses to dissuade predators; although antipredator compounds are more common in tropical seaweeds than in temperate zones, local algal species nevertheless produce a suite of chemical compounds. One such species, *Ulvaria obscura*, even produces dopamine—which we know as a human hormone and neurotransmitter, but which also deters growth in rival algal species.

LAND-SEA LINKAGES

If the shoreline is a border between land and water, it is a porous one. Tides rise and fall, fish foraging along the again-inundated ground. Seals haul out to sun themselves on rock. Rain washes soil downhill and into the sea, recycling sediment and nutrients. Great intertwinings of kelp break loose and wash up on beaches, new habitat for a community of terrestrial insects.

Land mammals often use the shoreline at mealtime, although we often don't think of them as beachgoers. Raccoons and deer pick their way among the boulders at low tide, feasting. Wolves do the same in British Columbia and Alaska. River otters sneak shoreward in broad daylight. Both grizzly and black bears forage for mussels and clams and other easy pickings between the tides (and the US government recognizes their Arctic cousin, the polar bear, as a marine mammal). Of course, these examples are all in addition to humans ourselves: we routinely eat shoreline species without thinking twice about being a linkage between land and sea.

The (nonhuman) mammals serve coastal ecosystems by moving nutrients out of the ocean and uphill onto land. These animals' droppings (and ultimately the bodies of the animals themselves) fertilize the trees and other plants of the coastal zone. Birds such as ospreys and eagles perform a similar function, hunting in the sea but making a home on land. And in the most spectacular example, the Pacific salmon runs (see Salmon and Humans in Western Washington in chapter 3, Washington's Puget Sound and Greater Salish Sea) move nutrients as far inland as Idaho. So the sea feeds the land, just as the land feeds the sea, rivers carrying away mountains bit by bit.

Perhaps, then, it's better to think of the shore as a border *region*—having some width, some content of its own—in which elements of land and sea overlap.

Facilitation: Benefitting One at No Cost to the Other

Even if competition and predation are the most obvious ways that species might influence one another, ecologists recognize a lot of subtler ways that the living parts of ecosystems influence what lives where.

Facilitation is the ecological term describing a situation in which one or both species benefit and neither is harmed. Facilitation can provide resources in the form of habitat, food, or refuge from predators or other stressors. By creating a more favorable or somehow different environment, such facilitation can increase species diversity in a given location.

For example, mussels can dominate parts of the intertidal, competing for space and ultimately crowding out other species looking for a solid rock to settle on. Yet mussels also can facilitate other species in this habitat by creating tiny hiding places between individual mussels that allow smaller animals to move in, hide from their predators, and escape the most direct forces of waves. And the mussel's shell is a hard surface that can mimic rock, providing space for attached organisms like barnacles

A predatory snail moves through a patch of barnacles. Sometimes known as a barnacle drill, the snail uses its radula to drill through the shells of its prey, then injects a digestive enzyme into the cavity and extracts the liquified tissues. A small barnacle rides on the shell of the snail, out of harm's way, while several limpets scour the snail's shell for microscopic algae; the snail provides habitat and food for these smaller species, an example of facilitation.

to settle and grow. In this case, the mere presence of mussels provides opportunity for scores of other invertebrates to make a home and a living.

LIFE AT THE OCEAN'S EDGE

Given the physical and biological challenges of intertidal life, why live between the tides at all? For starters, the edge of the ocean that lies against the coast is one of the most productive areas on the planet: the marriage of nutrient-rich water and sunlight provides fuel for phytoplankton and seaweeds that sustain small animals that filter, graze, or otherwise consume the productivity fed by the sun, in turn supporting entire food webs. And the intertidal zone offers space to settle, grow, and reproduce: rocks and cobbles, for example, create lots of places for species to attach or hide, and sandy habitats offer space for burrowing species. The diversity of intertidal habitats supports a diversity of life that is weird and wonderful and tailored to this highly variable environment.

Intertidal Zonation

The most striking ecological pattern in many coastal habitats is intertidal zonation—the regular, linear arrangement of species that progresses from high to low on the shore. This pattern is most obvious on vertical or sharply sloping faces and is perhaps the clearest illustration of ecological forces in tension.

The idea is that the lower habitat limits of a particular species are set by competition and predation, while upper limits are set by environmental forces such as temperature and desiccation. Mussels, for example, could tolerate environmental conditions lower on the shore, but in lower zones they are more vulnerable to predation by starfish and other predators. And

Seaweeds and invertebrates exhibit strong patterns of zonation, in which dominant species occupy specific horizontal bands in the intertidal. These patterns result from a combination of competition, predation, and environmental factors. Here, barnacles in the high intertidal zone give way to mussels in the mid intertidal zone and green algae in the lower intertidal zone.

mussels can't tolerate the heat and desiccation much farther up the shore. So they are where they are—restricted to a narrow band at a certain tidal height. Thus, the ultimate product of tides and waves and temperature, of competition and predation and a fair bit of chance, is a surprisingly consistent pattern visible all along the West Coast—and, indeed, worldwide.

The height—that is, the vertical extent—of these intertidal bands depends on tidal amplitude, increasing from south to north as the tidal amplitude increases. Other factors such as the slope or angle of the rock and exposure to waves and sun also play a role. And visitors may notice patterns even within an intertidal band: species with similar habitat requirements often partition space depending on who moved in first, who can hold space longest, and the vagaries of chance in the ongoing lottery for intertidal space.

Sand Becomes Habitat

Although it is not at all obvious, sandy habitats also often have subdivisions, zones akin to the more obvious zonation of the rocky intertidal. In the case of rocky intertidal zonation, a mix of species interactions and physical forces delimit the size and height of, say, the band of mussels running along shore. In the case of a sandy beach, it seems physical factors alone strongly influence what lives where. For example, lower-elevation habitats are saturated with water and host particular species of amphipods and polychaete worms, while relatively drier sand a few feet higher may harbor a completely different suite of small crustaceans, insects, and worms. In fact, sandy beaches even feature commuters, species that move up and down the beach with the tides—the mole crab is one of them. Taken together, a square yard of beach can support hundreds of thousands of small animals.

As a general rule, beaches with greater wave energy tend to be flatter in profile and to have finer-grained sand. These beaches also feature a far greater diversity of species than their coarser-grained steeper counterparts, for a few reasons. First, it seems that wave energy on the sand increases primary productivity via the growth of diatoms. More diatoms, in turn, support more diverse and larger food webs. Second, flatter

Sand can be quite different from place to place, as shown in this small selection of beach sand from around the world, part of a larger private collection. Courtesy of Dan and Ashley Reineman.

beaches have much longer swash periods—the time after a wave breaks during which the water flows back into the sea. Longer swash periods give suspension feeders a chance to eat in that thin layer of flowing water and also give waterborne individuals a chance to move around. A coarser-grained steeper beach will not support all of the small crustaceans and worms and others that require these conditions.

NAMING SPECIES

Since the time of Linnaeus in the mid-1700s, scientists have followed a convention for naming living things. The system is called binomial nomenclature, a somewhat fancy name for its recipe of identifying each species using two words. Even in the twenty-first century, those words are in Latin (or at least modified to look Latinate), because that was the international language of science for centuries. The result is a formal system of naming that is subject to humor and occasional ridicule but remains firmly in place.

Take, for example, the purple-ringed top snail, *Calliostoma annulatum*. *Calliostoma* is the genus, a group of closely related snail species, and it is a noun. The species name is an adjective describing that noun: *annulatum* refers to the particular species in question. The underlying idea is that scientific names reflect evolutionary relationships like a family tree: the species within a genus are all most closely related to one another. And each combination of genus and species names is unique, so those two words alone identify any species unambiguously. There is only one *C. annulatum*. Finally, as to style, scientists always capitalize genus names, never capitalize species names, and always italicize both.

Latin names are descriptive by design; they tell us something about the species itself if we can read some Latin. *Calliostoma* is a mash of Greek and Latin roots meaning "beautiful mouth or opening" and *annulatum* is straight-ahead Latin meaning "ringed." Hence, any species with the name *Calliostoma annulatum* had better be one good-looking snail—and indeed it is.

Latin names often describe the location where a species was first discovered or commonly lives (e.g., *Mytilus californianus*, the California mussel) or something about its shape (e.g., *Halosaccion glandiforme*, "salt sac" and "shaped like an acorn," describes a red seaweed) or sometimes the name of a person (e.g., *Laminaria setchellii*, a subtidal kelp named in honor of the prominent algal biologist William Albert Setchell). These names can even be inside jokes: although the blue whale, for example, is the largest animal on earth, its scientific name is *Balaenoptera*

The seaweed at left, whose Latin name, *Halosaccion glandiforme*, translates to "salt sac" and "shaped like an acorn," is one example of descriptive names; despite being classified as a red alga, it often loses its red appearance and takes on a yellowish or golden color.

musculus—*musculus* meaning "mouse." Giant kelp (*Macrocystis pyrifera*) has one of the better names meaning "great flaming balls." This refers to the flame-like blade emerging from each of its ball-like pneumatocysts (air bladders). And where scientists aren't sure what species they're referring to, they'll either abbreviate "species" as "sp." (or plural "spp.") or just use the genus name, as in "I slipped on some *Laminaria* and fell into a tidepool."

Scientific names can change for a few reasons. First, as new evidence comes to light, perhaps what had previously been classified as a single species becomes split into two or more. This happened commonly, for instance, when molecular techniques made it relatively easy to look at differences in DNA or proteins in different populations of a species. Most often, this splitting—or its opposite, lumping—changes the arrangement of species names within a genus.

Second, occasionally researchers will review the organization of names for a whole group of species. Because the organization of names should reflect their degrees of relatedness, when the understanding of the evolutionary relationships within a group changes, this may also change their names. Such reorganization might leave species names in place but change the genus or family name—for example, the red sea urchin went from being *Strongylocentrotus franciscanus* to being *Mesocentrotus franciscanus* during one such review. Naming priority also comes into play, as older names have priority over more recent ones, in an arcane series of rules maintained by the governing bodies of taxonomic nomenclature, which are as much fun as they sound.

Common names, in contrast to scientific names, don't follow strict rules and are almost always descriptive, though sometimes in ways that are hard to fathom. Purple urchin (*Strongylocentrotus purpuratus*) is a good example of a descriptive name: the urchin is clearly purple, unlike its cousins the red and green urchins. Rockweed is a descriptive name but somewhat less helpful: lots and lots of seaweeds grow on rocks, so choosing just one genus (*Fucus*) to call rockweed is a bit arbitrary. Other common names are applied to more than one species, often totally unrelated; for example, dead man's fingers is the common name of both the green seaweed *Codium fragile* and a terrestrial fungus that grows on decaying wood. The common name of the fat innkeeper (*Urechis caupo*) is one of those that stretches the imagination, though this worm does tend to be pudgy and does create burrows that host other species. And some intertidal species have no common name at all, or at least none that is widely used, forcing us to stick with the scientific name, however foreign it might sound.

3

The Salish Sea on a calm day

WASHINGTON'S PUGET SOUND AND GREATER SALISH SEA

On a map, Puget Sound and the greater Salish Sea look to be mere continuations of the Pacific Ocean, saltwater fingers poking into the North American landmass and similar to other bays and inlets along the coast. But this surface view is deceiving. In fact, several discrete, bathtub-like basins make up much of what we call Puget Sound. These basins are connected to the larger ocean via the Strait of Juan de Fuca, which is nearly a hundred miles long and forms the boundary between the US and Canada. The geographic separation between the Sound and the outer coastal waters creates an inland sea, a garden-like side circuit in which tides and currents mix oceanic water with rainwater and snowmelt running off of the surrounding mountain ranges.

Puget Sound has been the English name of this glacier-carved fjord since 1792, when George Vancouver named it in honor of Peter Puget, one of his lieutenants. But since the late twentieth century, the term Salish Sea—referring to the Salish Indigenous peoples of the region and encompassing Puget Sound, Georgia Strait, and the Strait of Juan de Fuca—has become common among those who live and work along its shores. Both Canadian and US geographic-naming authorities have officially accepted the newer term for the larger area, while Puget Sound remains the common term for the southern portions of the Salish Sea.

The area is home to thousands of marine and estuarine species—from iconic orcas, bald eagles, and salmon to seaweeds and segmented worms

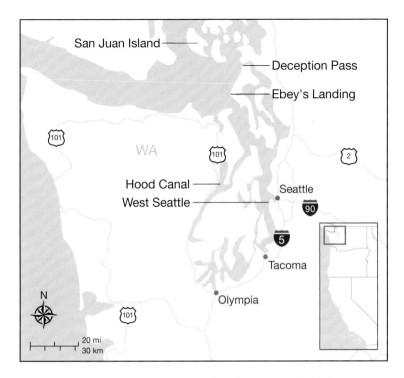

Featured locations in Washington's Puget Sound and greater Salish Sea

only a biologist could love. Migrating gray whales make annual stopovers in the Sound, as do growing numbers of humpback whales. Such abundant wildlife has long provided sustenance, recreation, ceremonial value, and commercial opportunity to the Sound's human population, which now includes millions of people.

Geologically, both land and sea in the Salish region are brand-new, having first been covered by a glacier nearly a mile thick, then exposed and altered as the glacier receded within the time frame of the earliest human occupation. Meltwater running *beneath* this glacier carved the north-south-trending troughs that make up Puget Sound. Glacial deposits formed sills, or barriers, creating sub-basins within Puget Sound, and each of the sub-basins has developed distinct characteristics: some are deeper, some are saltier, some are warmer, some are dynamic, some are sluggish. Consequently, despite its young geological age, Puget Sound's shores host a diversity of species across a range of habitats.

Most of Puget Sound's shoreline is protected from large waves and strong winds, with this protection reaching an extreme in the lazy, mud-filled bays of the south Sound. Soft-sediment creatures like clams and oysters tend to thrive here, as do many worms, shrimp, and other species that don't depend on the energy delivered by waves and wind. The result is a subtler kind of seashore ecology, but the curious visitor will nevertheless find rewards throughout the region.

PLACES TO EXPLORE
San Juan Islands

Even in a Pacific Northwest landscape full of superlatives, the San Juan Islands are an exceptionally picturesque group of moss-clad rocks, graced by madrone and Douglas fir. In the rain shadow of the Olympics, the San Juans get slightly more than half the rainfall of Seattle (and only one-sixth that of the famously dreary Forks). At more protected sites, the quiet of small waves lapping against the rocky shore is broken only by the occasional ferry; in more exposed areas, winter storms pile wave-borne logs on the beach.

Here the international border tiptoes around the San Juans in a curious way, with the result that the archipelago lies within the boundaries of the US, while the Canadian city of Victoria, British Columbia, lies noticeably south of most points in the San Juans. The effect is a serpentine western edge to the very long and mostly straight border that runs from the Great Lakes to Puget Sound. For this squiggle we owe Kaiser Wilhelm of Germany, who resolved a border dispute between the US and Canada in 1872, finding in favor of the US and rendering San Juan Island the last site of British occupation in the country.

The shores of the San Juan Islands are more marine than estuarine, although freshwater from British Columbia's Fraser River can lower salinity considerably, especially in the northern reaches of the archipelago (see Salinity in chapter 2, Living between the Tides). Vancouver Island protects much of the island habitat from the real violence of Pacific

The San Juan Archipelago consists of more than 400 islands and islets in the Salish Sea.

waves, and so the coastal fauna is a mix of marine species that tend to do well in the absence of large waves while being able to tolerate warm temperatures during daytime low tides in summer.

The San Juans may be best known as a place to see Southern Resident killer whales, more commonly referred to as orcas (see Species of Interest later in this chapter). The whales are frequently seen in the summer months, especially along the west side of San Juan Island, but can be spotted year-round throughout the islands and even south into Puget Sound. Within the San Juans, visitors often go to Lime Kiln Point State Park on San Juan Island to see orcas passing through Haro Strait.

CATTLE POINT AREA, SAN JUAN ISLAND

Cattle Point forms the southernmost stub of land on San Juan Island. The name, it appears, comes from an episode in the 1850s during which a vessel transporting livestock to the nearby Hudson's Bay Company farm foundered, forcing the cattle to swim to shore. Although the cattle are long gone, the area still boasts expansive grasslands covering marine terraces—wave-cut benches left behind as former glaciers retreated. A fringe of rocky intertidal habitat interspersed with beaches of cobble and sand occupies the shoreline here. Most of the area lies within San Juan Islands National Historical Park and Washington State's adjacent Natural Resources Conservation Area. A lighthouse sits atop Cattle Point, poised over the entrance to Cattle Pass and serving as a historical aid to navigation for ships transiting the eastern Strait of Juan de Fuca.

A red alga (*Palmaria mollis*) is common here, recognizable by its deep red color and vaguely V-shaped blade, much narrower at the base than at the tip. On Atlantic coasts, where *Palmaria* also grows, it is often known as dulse and has been eaten for centuries. Fittingly, the genus name comes

A large boulder below the Cattle Point lighthouse is a glacial erratic, a reminder of transport and deposition by glaciers. In the foreground, a bright orange lichen adds a colorful hue to the upper intertidal rocks. The lower intertidal at Cattle Point consists of a rock bench with cobbles and sand.

from "palm-shaped." Confirm its identity by the sound(!) this seaweed makes: when torn from top to bottom, blades of *Palmaria mollis* make an audible ripping noise that other red seaweeds don't. To hear this, you have to hold the blade very close to your ear; you will not be the first to look silly doing this.

Along the bluff trail, looking seaward and depending on the state of sea and tide, Salmon Bank comes into view. This feature is a relatively shallow underwater extension of rocky landform that for more than a century was an important location for catching salmon. In summer, squabbles of gulls converge on Salmon Bank to feed on aggregations of forage fish. Along the same trail, you're likely to see bald eagles overhead or perched on large boulders surveying the surroundings. Northern harriers fly low over the grasslands searching for their rodent prey. And special treats await the winter visitor: golden eagles and short-eared owls both can be sighted then.

The bluff trail leads to South Beach, which, at more than two miles in length, is the longest public beach on the island. The western section of South Beach is covered with driftwood of varying sizes and ages. The really big pieces of driftwood have diameters of a yard or more and could date back to the early 1900s or even earlier. These large pieces tend to be stable, moving around only with the largest storm tides, while the smaller pieces tend to come and go more frequently (see Wave Action, Exposure, and Disturbance in chapter 2, Living between the Tides).

Toward the east end of South Beach, the amount of driftwood declines and the width of the beach narrows, being hemmed in by an eroding steep bluff. On the beach below the bluff sit large boulders that long ago were deposited by glaciers in the sediments on the bluff top and that, over time, have ended up on the beach as the bluff eroded. Sandy beach yields to fringing bedrock and the tidepools within. This rocky area at the very eastern tip of South Beach experiences vigorous tidal mixing and the full force of storms in winter as waves build along the length of the Strait of Juan de Fuca.

The intertidal biota at Cattle Point reflects the level of exposure here, which is intermediate between the truly wave-exposed sites of the outer coast and the more protected inland waters of Puget Sound. Here lives the large California mussel (*Mytilus californianus*), which is abundant on Washington's wave-swept outer coast but is missing from more protected waters, as well as a gooseneck barnacle (see Species of Interest in chapter 4, Washington's Outer Coast), also common on exposed shores with vigorous wave action. At the same time, abundant stands of rockweed (see Species of Interest in chapter 4), which are common throughout the sheltered waters of the San Juans, are obvious along the tide line, together with filamentous seaweeds that do well in calm waters.

ICEBERG POINT, LOPEZ ISLAND

Some of the richest rocky intertidal habitat in the San Juans is found at Iceberg Point. Sitting at the south end of Lopez Island, Iceberg Point shares many characteristics with Cattle Point, which lies within sight across Middle Channel and the entrance to Cattle Pass. The rocky landforms of Iceberg Point, combined with exposure to the waves and wind of the Strait of Juan de Fuca, provide habitat for animals and seaweeds that are more typical of outer-coastal sites. The relatively steep bathymetry—the sharp drop-off close to shore—offers good habitat for foraging seabirds, seals, and sea lions.

The dynamic nature of this shoreline is immediately apparent from the storm-cast logs high in the intertidal. The lower intertidal is covered by the stipeless kelp (*Hedophyllum sessile*), also unaccountably known as sea cabbage, although it doesn't look like a cabbage at all. Sea cabbage gives way to surfgrass (*Phyllospadix* spp.), which is typical of wave-swept shores. Surfgrass—a true plant (not a seaweed)—is unusual among plants in that it attaches directly to rocky substrates instead of using roots buried in sediment to hold itself in place. Coralline algae (see Species of Interest in chapter 6, The Southern Oregon Coast), pinkish seaweeds with calcium carbonate in their cell walls, are abundant here.

You'll often find the aggregating anemone (*Anthopleura elegantissima*) growing alongside coralline algae. Some of the nutrition of this clonal anemone comes from an algal symbiont that, through an elegant relationship, supplies carbohydrates to the anemone via photosynthesis.

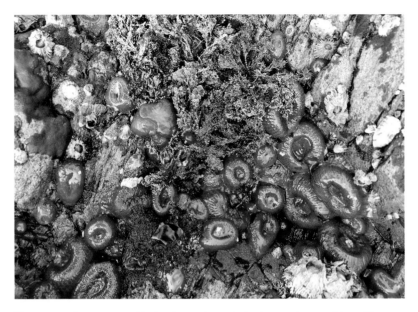

The aggregating anemone (*Anthopleura elegantissima*) grows here amid coralline algae, barnacles, and limpets. The green color of this anemone indicates that it hosts photosynthetic microalgae in its outer cell layers. The clonal nature of this species allows it to achieve very high densities in some areas.

While able to reproduce sexually, these clonal anemones often reproduce by fission, splitting one into two and again into four, to produce the aggregates you see on the shore. Where two different clones meet, they will sometimes use specialized cells to mount defenses against each other, presumably in a bid to hold space. This species also produces alarm pheromones that are released when an individual is wounded, causing other individuals to retract in defense. The chemical signaling even works across species, a remarkable example of communication in the world of invertebrates.

On a summer's day when the sun is out and the tide is low, bubbles may emerge from the greenish waters of the higher tidepools. These bubbles are the product of photosynthesis, with algae cranking out oxygen in high gear when sunlight is abundant and the pools warm. This is a sign of oxygen production that much of the time isn't easily observable.

Sounds drift from across the water: on foggy days, perhaps only foghorns, while on sunny days the calls of sea lions and seabirds ring out. Iceberg Point features a long list of marine birds–grebes, cormorants, mergansers, scoters, oystercatchers, phalaropes, murres, murrelets, auklets, guillemots, and a host of gull species, plus others–offering evidence of the good feeding habitat the area provides.

Even more alluring than bird calls, at least to some, are the calls of the Steller sea lion (see Marine Mammals in chapter 6, The Southern Oregon Coast), which is sometimes spotted in the area. Stellers tend to roar rather than bark and so can sound more like bears than the more familiar California sea lions (see Marine Mammals in chapter 6). Sea lions use the nearby offshore islets as haul-outs but aren't known to breed or rear pups inside Puget Sound.

Deception Pass

Geologically, Deception Pass is the approximate dividing line between the exposed bedrock beaches of Fidalgo Island and the San Juans, and the sediment-laden shores to the south. A Depression-era bridge spans the turbulent water 180 feet below, and Deception Pass State Park is a popular destination for Northwesterners as well as visitors.

From the perspective of those who live on land, Deception Pass is a narrow channel separating Whidbey Island (to the south) from Fidalgo Island (to the north). But from the watery perspective of marine life, Deception Pass unites rather than divides. The passage links the Strait of Juan de Fuca with Skagit Bay and Possession Sound, which form part of the larger Whidbey Basin. Twice-daily tides move huge volumes of water through the narrow Deception Pass, resulting in swift currents that carry a great deal of tidal energy. Wave energy, too, coming in from the Strait of Juan de Fuca, is greater than is typical for most areas in the Salish Sea.

The sub-basins on either side of the pass feature notably different habitats, and not simply because the energetic regimes differ between the east and west sides of the pass. Waters to the west are more oceanic, are colder, and have higher salinity. Waters to the east are generally warmer

The Deception Pass Bridge links Whidbey and Fidalgo Islands in Washington State.

A bevy of black katy chitons (*Katharina tunicata*) hangs tight at Deception Pass. These molluscs are normally found in high-wave-energy environments, and their appearance here is a hint that Deception Pass is a higher-energy spot than most places within the relatively protected Salish Sea.

Seaweeds are abundant in the calm bays near Deception Pass.

and fresher, diluted by the output of substantial rivers—the Skagit, and to some extent the Stillaguamish and Snohomish. Hence, on the outer shores of Deception Pass we find rocky substrates covered with a community of seaweeds and invertebrates that looks not too different from those typical of rocky sites in the Strait of Juan de Fuca, while a short distance away, at Cornet Bay inside Deception Pass, quiet beaches of soft sediment support a radically different suite of species living within the sediment, such as worms and clams.

One of the more accessible shorelines here is on the north side of Deception Pass at Rosario Beach. The trail from the parking lot leads down to Rosario Head, a chunk of durable ancient seabed that is presently tied to the mainland by a narrow finger of accumulated sediment. To the north of the head is Rosario Beach and to the south and east is the far-more-protected Sharpe Cove. These sites make apparent the large difference that a degree of wave exposure makes: while Rosario Beach is composed of small cobbles, the cove is muddier and gives the distinct impression that it might lie undisturbed for long stretches of time. There's also a difference in the amount and size of the accumulated driftwood, with more and larger pieces resting on Rosario Beach than in Sharpe Cove. Differences in wave energy between the two sites are why there is a boat dock at Sharpe Cove and not at Rosario Beach.

Rosario Head itself supplies the rock for the local rocky intertidal habitat, and as is almost always the case, the rocks and pools nearest the trail-access point bear the brunt of abuse by visitors.

Eelgrass beds occur in quiet areas around Deception Pass. These beds tend to be small and sparse—nothing like the broad expanse of eelgrass that can be found just to the north in Padilla Bay. But in these eelgrass beds lie treasures of an unusual sort: the stalked jellyfish (*Haliclystus* and *Manania* spp.). Stalked jellies are true jellyfish that live attached to eelgrass and seaweeds. And, curiously, these attached forms are medusae, equivalent to the umbrella-shaped, free-swimming medusae familiar to beachgoers. Different from typical medusae, whose long tentacles dangle in the water to capture prey, the short tentacles of stalked jellies are arranged to catch small invertebrates such as amphipods. And even though stalked jellies appear firmly fixed to their host plant (or seaweed), they can use their stalk to glide short distances.

Ebey's Landing, Whidbey Island

Sand and other kinds of sediment are in constant motion at the shore: the particular grains of sand on one beach on a given day will be swept away by currents and deposited elsewhere in short order. Sediment erodes away from some coastal areas (sources) and flows toward and is deposited in others (sinks). The feeder bluffs of Puget Sound are sources of sediment, constantly eroding and providing sediment that stabilizes (feeds) beaches elsewhere. Around Puget Sound, many beaches are backed by feeder bluffs that vary in size, from low vegetated banks to towering cliffs of sediment that is easily eroded into the Sound.

Ebey's Landing hosts an unusual lagoon habitat at the base of the bluffs. Perego's Lagoon sits between a low sandy barrier and the beach

Ebey's Landing on Whidbey Island is a landscape shaped by glaciers and the clay, silt, sand, and gravel that they leave behind. The steep slopes of shoreline bluffs are the glacial equivalents of highway road cuts, supplying sediment via wind and water erosion to Puget Sound. Nearby, Perego's Lagoon offers an example of an unusual coastal feature.

itself. The sandy barrier stands seaward of the original coastline and is created and maintained by long-shore transport of sediment, in this case from eroding bluffs to the north of the lagoon. The low barrier is occasionally breached by large waves associated with storms, creating overwash. When this happens, the incoming water replenishes the lagoon and deposits new sediment. Despite occasional replenishment, the water in Perego's Lagoon can be warmer and saltier than the adjacent waters of Admiralty Inlet. And although Jakle's and Third Lagoons on San Juan Island were formed by the same processes as Perego's Lagoon, Perego's differs in being shallower and more exposed to the weather. Facing west to the open Strait of Juan de Fuca, Perego's is fully exposed to sun on hot summer days and to wind and wave action in winter. Consequently, despite their similar geological origins, the lagoons on San Juan Island and at Ebey's Landing differ in the biological life that they support.

Pigeon guillemots (*Cepphus columba*), easy to spot with their red feet and black and white plumage, often nest high on rocky cliffs above the water or in burrows on eroding bluff faces.

The bluffs of Whidbey Island are favored nesting habitat for the pigeon guillemot (see Birds of the Exposed Coast in chapter 5, The Northern Oregon Coast). They nest in cliff-side burrows and crevices in spots that are protected from predators. From their burrows they launch themselves toward the water to forage by diving and swimming, returning to the burrow with a bill full of wriggling fish to present to their young. Simply watching the birds come and go from their burrows is great fun—they leave their burrows by descending steeply along the cliff face to generate the lift required for flight. On their return, they do the opposite, approaching the burrow from below and then ascending sharply to land feetfirst on the burrow's lip. Breeding colonies are scattered around Puget Sound, including a colony near Fort Casey just south of Ebey's Landing, one of more than two dozen pigeon guillemot colonies on Whidbey Island. Activity peaks in the summer, especially in the morning when the birds are feeding hungry chicks.

FLOATS AND PILINGS

A good low tide isn't always necessary to get a good view of intertidal life. Floats and pilings provide man-made real estate for many marine species, in essence creating miniature artificial reefs that support a community of invertebrates, seaweeds, and fishes.

These habitats can differ sharply from those in surrounding natural areas: the substrates often are vertical instead of horizontal and typically are composed of concrete or creosote-soaked wood rather than rock and sand. The overwater structures tend to create shade, limiting the amount of light that penetrates the water, and the in-water structures can alter water motion and sediment deposition. Docks and pilings are areas of high human activity, especially boating, which can further modify the environment.

Mussels and barnacles make good use of artificial substrates such as those provided by docks and pilings. Less evident from the surface is the diversity of subtidal species that cling to these structures. The undersides of floating docks in protected marinas can be particularly rich.

Despite these differences, suspension-feeding invertebrates do well on these surfaces, as do some seaweeds. Grazers and predators move in to take advantage of the food supply, and others are drawn to the array of microhabitats that form as the community develops.

The species that live on floats and pilings tend to be a subset of those that inhabit nearby waters. Frequently, though, these structures attract nonnative species that can become invasive; for example, in parts of Puget Sound, invasive tunicates (also known as sea squirts) can occur in high abundance on floats, to the exclusion of native species.

West Seattle

It's possible to do some intertidal exploring within sight of downtown Seattle. In the span of about a mile, a mosaic of microhabitats reflects the tight connections between land, sea, and human use, providing a vivid example of how these environments can change over small spatial scales.

West Seattle sits on a peninsula, created from glacial till, that sticks out into Puget Sound and forms the western boundary of Elliott Bay. From West Seattle's eastern shoreline, the view of Seattle's skyline is unparalleled. Yet this view also reveals a marine environment shaped by the massive fingerprint of humankind. Downtown skyscrapers line the shore across the bay; one of the busiest US maritime ports lies just to the south; and a stretch of riprap keeps the shore of Elliott Bay rigidly in place, buffering the wake of enormous cargo ships going to and from the port. The signature of human beings is everywhere.

That human presence is part of what makes this site interesting. The influence of urban and industrial activity has altered the ecology of the place well beyond its natural state, yet marine communities persist in recognizable ways.

Downtown Seattle as seen from West Seattle, reflecting the intersection of marine and urban environments. Rock rubble and concrete are often used to harden shorelines to guard against erosion and storm surge, and although few humans find it attractive, many marine species call these hard surfaces home. "Weedy" species— ecological generalists that tolerate a wide range of conditions, reproduce quickly, and disperse widely—are likely to show up in such human-dominated spaces, and the diversity of species in urban areas can be surprisingly high.

The east-facing hardened shorelines are in some sense rocky but are a departure from the kinds of natural habitats that seaweeds and invertebrates typically inhabit. Combine differences in substrate with the comings and goings of boat traffic and the toxic Superfund site on the nearby Duwamish River, and a picture of ecological stress emerges. Among the riprap, tidepools occupy the interstitial spaces, loaded mostly with barnacles and an anemone or two, limpets and chitons here and there. The diversity of intertidal life typical in the Pacific Northwest is largely absent.

Around the bend at the north end of the peninsula is a long sand beach with a shallow slope. The fine sand grains provide a home for burrowing animals like clams and worms, but there's not much solid ground here to

A spaghetti worm (family Terebellidae)—removed from its tube of sand, shell fragments, and mucus—shows off the tangle of dark reddish-brown feeding tentacles that inspire its common name. Its tube can be many inches long, glued to the underside of rocks and often found at low tide by visitors turning over medium-sized rocks. Look for tiny pea crabs (*Pinnixa* spp.) or scale worms (family Polynoidae) that also make their homes in these tubes.

attach to. Around the bend on the southwest-facing part of the peninsula, a shelf of bedrock offers more diversity.

Facing into Puget Sound proper, this rocky shelf provides a relatively flat and accessible window into urban intertidal life. On good low tides, a beach naturalist from the Seattle Aquarium will set up shop here, answering questions and pointing out the seaweeds and invertebrates. The shore here, known as Me-Kwa-Mooks Natural Area, tends to support the kinds of marine life we find in other protected parts of Puget Sound, including chitons and limpets, anemones and sea stars, crabs and small fishes. One of the most brightly colored animals in lower-energy environments such as this is the orange sea cucumber (*Cucumaria miniata*), holding fast between the rocks with its legion of tube feet. When submerged, it extends its brightly colored orange tentacles to feed, forming a wide net to catch plankton and organic debris. Flatworms, polychaete worms, clams, and small crustaceans such as isopods and shore crabs are also abundant.

Hood Canal

Despite its name, Hood Canal is not a canal at all. It is instead a glacier-carved arm of Puget Sound, a long, skinny fjord that points southwest like a giant harpoon. Conditions at the mouth of Hood Canal are driven by relatively cold, saline ocean water entering from the Strait of Juan de Fuca. Farther south in the canal, freshwater runoff from multiple rivers dilutes the salt water significantly, creating an environmental gradient of water conditions. Medium-energy beaches near the mouth give way to low-energy beaches farther south, and a distinct estuary occupies Hood Canal's southernmost reaches, where water motion is sluggish and water temperatures can rise sharply. Tides flush Hood Canal incompletely, and consequently the amount of oxygen in the water can run critically low at some times of year. Primary productivity is relatively high throughout Hood Canal, especially in spring and summer. Communities typical of sand and gravel habitats dominate the shores.

US Highway 101 runs along the western edge of Hood Canal, just along the water at the base of the Olympic Mountains. The terrain of the Olympic Peninsula rises steeply to the west, leaving little room for human development—towns along the canal are tiny and far-between, and most of the human activity lies right along the highway.

The fjord's entrance features a mix of sand and mud on either side of the Hood Canal Bridge, one of the world's longest floating bridges. It is generally a calm place, protected by geography from serious wave action coming from the Strait of Juan de Fuca. Low tide at Shine Tidelands State Park (or the equivalent site on the eastern side of the bridge, Salisbury Point County Park) reveals a shallow beach strewn with cobble. This site offers a good introduction to the habitats of Hood Canal more generally, in that much of the biodiversity lies below the surface. Clams and oysters are abundant here. Dungeness crabs and kelp crabs forage in the shallows, and bits of seaweed and eelgrass drift in with the tide, providing food for permanently attached animals that have found purchase on the odd rock. Worms inhabit shallow sediments throughout Hood Canal, though they tend to be inconspicuous.

Major and minor rivers drain the Olympic Mountains, creating deltas where they meet the canal's shore. The deltas can be expansive, supporting a host of species that live on the sediment's surface (epifauna) and others that live within the sediment (infauna). While some species of seaweed are commonly found here—for instance, sea lettuce (*Ulva* spp.) and the rockweed *Fucus distichus*—invertebrates are far more conspicuous. On the surface, shelled animals are abundant: Pacific oysters, mussels, barnacles, snails, and limpets. A bit of digging will produce clams of various species in addition to soft-bodied invertebrates, many of which are worms that are unidentifiable except by a handful of experts.

In other areas along the canal, where deltas haven't built broad tidelands, the shore can be comparatively narrow and steeply sloping. These sites can be backed by rock formations and typically consist of cobble beaches occupied by many of the same shelled species found on the deltaic beaches.

A comparatively narrow beach toward the southern end of Hood Canal is covered in oysters, barnacles, mussels, and rockweed, typical of such sheltered environments.

Mudflats such as those found around Hood Canal—indeed, around all of Puget Sound—can be smelly places due to the release of hydrogen sulfide (see Energy in chapter 2, Living between the Tides). It's likely that our aversion to the smell of hydrogen sulfide is related to its toxicity, though a visit to a mudflat is unlikely to cause any harm. Decaying algae, too, can give off hydrogen sulfide, sometimes in deadly amounts (see Sea Lettuce, below).

State parks dot the edges of Hood Canal at regular intervals, offering ready access to the shore. Dosewallips, Potlatch, and Twanoh State Parks are the largest of these, each with acres of shoreline to explore. Locals commonly dig for clams at these and other areas along Hood Canal, and stores statewide sell permits to do so.

SPECIES OF INTEREST

Turkish Towel

This bumpy red alga is supposedly reminiscent of the towels from a Turkish bath, hence its common name Turkish towel (*Chondracanthus exasperatus*); its Latin name is nearly as evocative: *Chondracanthus* means "cartilaginous spines," and *exasperatus* here means "rough." It is sometimes confused with the smaller *Mastocarpus papillatus*, known by extension as Turkish washcloth.

Turkish towel's striking texture and large size make it quite recognizable, and washed-up blades can become curiosities for beachgoers. Blades can be up to twenty inches long and tend to grow rapidly with abundant summer sunlight. Native to Puget Sound, it tolerates a wide range of temperatures, enabling it to live as far south as Baja California.

Bull Kelp

Also known as bullwhip kelp, bull kelp (*Nereocystis leutkeana*) is a common sight on beaches of the Pacific Northwest. Easy to identify, bull kelp consists of a holdfast; a long, hollow stipe of up to sixty feet; a single large air bladder or float; and a tangle of long blades. Bull kelp lives in the subtidal zone and plays an important role in nearshore systems by providing habitat for fish, invertebrates, and other seaweeds, as well as food for grazers and abundant beach wrack.

Forests of bull kelp (*Nereocystis leutkeana*) are prominent in more exposed areas of Puget Sound.

Bright-green sea lettuce (*Ulva* sp.) stands out against pink anemones. The seaweed's thin blades are just two cells thick, fragile and easily torn. Sea lettuce occupies calm-water habitats worldwide.

Sea Lettuce

Sea lettuce (*Ulva* spp.) is a splash of bright green on the low tide in waters where nutrients are abundant, such as quiet bays, river mouths, and even sewer outfalls. It's common along the US West Coast and around the world, eaten by invertebrates and sometimes humans.

Where nutrient pollution is severe, *Ulva* can accumulate in quantities so large they are referred to as green tides, and this can become a public health hazard—although not along the US West Coast, where the alga doesn't reach such high abundances. Rotting *Ulva* produces hydrogen sulfide, a toxic gas, and stepping on a crust of decomposing algae can release a toxic plume. Although this is rarely harmful to humans along the West Coast, elsewhere people and even horses are known to have been overwhelmed: in Europe in 2009, a horse and rider trudged into a mass of rotting *Ulva* several feet thick, releasing sulfur dioxide gas. The horse collapsed and died, and the unconscious rider was dragged to safety.

Eelgrass

Greenery in marine environments generally tends to be created by seaweeds instead of true plants. An important exception is eelgrass (*Zostera marina*), one of the very few honest-to-goodness flowering plants that lives in salt water. Eelgrass grows throughout the northern hemisphere in shallow marine habitats protected from strong wave action, planting roots in soft sediments and forming dense meadows of bright-green leaves that wave with the tide.

These plants lack the architecture to support their own weight in the absence of water, and so low tide finds the leaves splayed on the sediment. Floating packets of pollen fertilize eelgrass flowers at the water's surface, and remarkably, the species also produces strings of submarine pollen that can fertilize flowers underwater. Eelgrass seeds disperse by water motion instead of by wind or by animal vectors, and some are even endowed with small gas bubbles that help the seeds float away.

Quite apart from its successful adaptations to the marine environment, eelgrass has outsize ecological importance: when the tide is up, the plant creates three-dimensional structure that soft-sediment habitats otherwise lack. Eelgrass roots and rhizomes stabilize intertidal sediments, while the leaves slow water motion and shelter juvenile fishes and invertebrates of many sorts. An array of associated species grows upon the leaves themselves, creating miniature ecosystems of epiphytes and grazers. Fine silt settles out from the water that is slowed by eelgrass leaves, creating

Wedged into a narrow band between broad mudflat and sea, eelgrass (*Zostera marina*) grows at the mouth of False Bay on San Juan Island. Gulls take advantage of the low tide to forage.

habitat that favors clams, worms, and other invertebrates. The leaves grow rapidly and then die back seasonally, washing up on beaches, where the wrack of dead eelgrass becomes habitat for amphipods, flies, beetles, and other invertebrates.

Jellyfish

At the risk of stating the obvious, jellyfish are neither fish nor jelly. They are instead animals that are nearly as different from a fish as it is possible to be, members of a group called cnidarians. The group consists of generally squishy animals that tend to be radially symmetrical and armed with tiny harpoon-like stinging cells. Anemones and corals are in the same group. And, indeed, it makes sense to think of jellies as carnivorous upside-down anemones, stinging tentacles trailing out below the animal's main body.

In fact, most jellyfish species alternate body forms with each generation: the familiar bell-shaped jelly (the medusa) gives rise to a stationary, attached form (the polyp) resembling its anemone relatives. Then, in a move straight out of a movie featuring space aliens, the polyp cuts off small buds that eventually turn into tiny, independent medusae. It's truly wild.

The familiar medusa phase of most jellies is planktonic. They are active swimmers, by virtue of the muscular bell that contracts rhythmically to propel them upward, countering a tendency to sink. Many have primitive eyespots that can at minimum tell light from dark, and some may even process images, which is quite a trick in the absence of a central nervous system. And as a group, jellyfish have been around at least 750 million years, a testament to the durability of their seemingly simple body plan and life-history strategy.

In the Pacific Northwest, we commonly see jellies at the water's surface or stranded on beaches in summer, when they are most numerous. The most prevalent species in these waters include two with harsh stings: the sea nettle (*Chrysaora fuscescens*) and the lion's mane (*Cyanea capillata*), the latter of which can be over six feet across the bell, with a credible claim to being the world's largest species of jellyfish. And yes, the tentacles can sting you even if you find the animal washed up dead on the beach.

The crystal jelly (*Aequorea victoria*) bears many radiating ribs and is bioluminescent around its outer margin, but it's almost invisible both in the water and on the beach, where beachwalkers often see it as they're about to step on it. Totally transparent and lacking in any color, it looks like a large gelatinous magnifying glass. The graceful moon jellies (*Aurelia* spp.), quite distant relatives that can be common in less-exposed waters, are recognizable by four horseshoe-shaped gonads visible through the translucent bell.

The fried-egg jelly (*Phacellophora camtschatica*) bears an almost-comical resemblance to its namesake breakfast food, and it may carry with it crustaceans that use its bell for shelter. You can often see these on Washington State ferry crossings.

Finally, and also only distantly related to the true jellies, *Velella velella* is a remarkable story in natural history. This cerulean-blue-and-transparent species lives at the very interface between ocean and air, with

In life, the crystal jelly (*Aequorea victoria*) is a free-swimming, bioluminescent jellyfish. When it's washed up on shore, the radiating ribs around its bell may still be visible.

gas-filled pockets in its body that help keep it there. Out of the water sticks a sail: a fin of tissue that catches the wind and propels the animal along—hence, its common name, the by-the-wind sailor. It lives in oceans worldwide, a single cosmopolitan species... and most weirdly, each individual *Velella* is in fact a colony of smaller individuals called hydroids.

Given that by-the-wind sailors catch the wind but have no means of steering, certain wind conditions can drive *Velella* onto beaches by the thousands. After a few days, beachgoers find their gelatinous discs crisped in the sun, stranded voyagers from the open seas.

Sponges and Tunicates

Low down in the intertidal zone, under a rocky overhang, blotches of color can blanket the rocky surface. These blotches are probably either sponges or tunicates, two radically different kinds of animals that have evolved vaguely similar lifestyles.

Sponges are familiar from the tropical examples that find their way into bathtubs everywhere, but local species tend to have low growth profiles more akin to a crust on low-intertidal rocks. Those crusts are slightly spongy to the touch and sport an irregular set of raised bumps, each bump having a single opening through which the sponge takes in water for food and performs life's other necessary functions. Along West Coast shores, sponges can be pink or purple or beige (or other colors), and although they may not even strike you as animals at all, they're incredibly efficient eaters, filtering up to 99 percent of plankton in their target size range. And despite having the most primitive body plans in the animal kingdom, they nevertheless sport bits of calcium carbonate—or even glass—that firm up the body wall and deter predators.

Tunicates are at the opposite end of the animal tree of life, and despite all appearances, they are some of our closest relatives in the tidepools. Tunicates belong to the group of animals called chordates, which includes everything with a dorsal nerve cord, from fish to humans. Adult tunicates look nothing like vertebrates, but the giveaway is earlier in development: tunicates have a larval stage that looks quite like a tadpole, and adults have lost many of the features that make the larvae recognizable as our relatives.

Different species of tunicate can look quite different from each other, but along our shores, those that live in colonies, such as those in the photo at right, are among the most conspicuous. Colonial tunicates frequently live alongside sponges in low-intertidal habitats protected from the sun, often in colors of bright orange or pink. They feel a bit slippery and almost rubbery, with a translucent outer layer (the "tunic") made of cellulose, a material far more closely associated with plants than animals. Solitary tunicates, those that don't form colonies, are known as sea squirts, and although they look quite different, they are found in similar habitats.

In other regions, larger forms of tunicates and sponges are notable. Impressive specimens of both groups can be found in tropical waters— for example, the giant barrel sponges of Caribbean reefs. One genus of tropical tunicates called *Pyrosoma* can form huge tube-shaped colonies that swim through the water column emitting a bluish light. These are large enough to show up on radar, and indeed there is some evidence these tunicates were perceived as enemy torpedoes during the Gulf of

A bright-red sponge (upper center-left) and an orange colonial tunicate (center-right) create a riot of unexpected color under a shaded overhang.

Tonkin incident that led the US into the Vietnam War. It was a rare case of a marine invertebrate playing a role in international hostilities.

Bryozoans

A patch of pale white on a large kelp blade or a translucent glob with a hint of internal structure on rocks low in the intertidal may catch the eye of the curious visitor. Or perhaps it's a feathery, almost algal-looking thing under rocky overhangs. In each case, the object of curiosity is likely a colony of bryozoans, tiny animals whose colonies can take a wide variety of forms, some of which are quite common along our shores. These are interesting creatures in tiny packages, and because they are small we generally recognize them by the shapes of their colonies rather than by the individuals themselves.

Entertainingly, *bryozoa* means "moss animals," which gives a good sense of what to look for: colonies consist of many small semi-independent individuals, each called a zooid. Within a colony, zooids specialize to take on feeding, defensive, reproductive, or other functions, making the colony a sort of superorganism. Feeding zooids typically filter food out of the surrounding water using a veil of small tentacles, which they can retract into a durable body wall.

Ribbon Worms

Not all worm-shaped things are worms. Or, rather, the animal kingdom has come up with worm-shaped body plans many times, and the earthworm that springs to mind is only one of many (essentially unrelated) skinny, limbless examples. In marine and estuarine environments, there are indeed many earthworm relatives, but alongside them live a quite different set of species: the fearsome ribbon worms (in the *Amphiporus*, *Emplectonema*, and *Paranemertes* genera, to name just a few). If you happen upon a two-foot-long string of bright orange under an intertidal rock or find a smooth purple creature with crosswise markings like a ruler, you have found a ribbon worm.

These fierce hunters stalk soft-bodied prey up to—and even exceeding—their own size, using a potent weapon: a tubular mouthpart called a proboscis that they shoot out of an opening at or near their mouth. The proboscis, which may be nearly the length of the ribbon worm's body, packs either sticky mucous or a sharp piercing implement called a stylet. Having pierced the unfortunate prey's body wall, the stylet then delivers paralytic venom. Handily, a supply of replacement stylets awaits use in a nearby sac. Having paralyzed its prey, the worm then hauls the victim in for digestion.

So to review, many of these animals carry around a set of toxic darts on a huge internal organ they can launch out of their bodies to stab, paralyze, and recover unduly large prey. Pretty impressive for a "worm."

Moon Snail

The moon snail (*Neverita lewisii*, formerly *Polinices lewisii*, named for Meriwether Lewis of the Lewis and Clark expedition) is the largest snail you're likely to see in these waters, plying the lower reaches of soft-bottom habitats in search of clams and other invertebrates to eat. Moon

Moon snails (*Neverita lewisii*) are reigning monarchs of the region's slow-moving molluscs. Amazingly, they can entirely retract their oversize foot into their shell when prompted, expelling a large amount of water in the process. Photo by Stacey Vaeth.

snails are nighttime hunters, preying on other molluscs by wrapping their muscular large foot around the prey's shell. It's a predatory bulldozer of a mollusc, parting the sediment as it feels its way along the bottom, its softball-sized shell dwarfed by a foot splaying outward in every direction. After drilling through a clam shell with its radula and consuming the soft tissue, a moon snail leaves behind the empty shell bearing a distinctive circular hole with beveled edges.

During the warmer months, visitors are far more likely to see the moon snail's egg cases than the snail itself, although they might not be immediately recognizable as such. In reproducing, females use mucus to bind together sand grains in a ring around their shells. They release eggs onto this sandy ring or collar, then finally lay down another layer of sand over the eggs, embedding the eggs in a sandy sandwich. The snails extrude the mixture in a curl around their bodies to produce a distinctive, durable collar. The finished egg case can be several inches across and to some observers resembles an old-fashioned shirt collar or a bit of oddly shaped debris. The eggs hatch after about six weeks, off to seek their fortunes in the world.

Geoduck

In the world of clams, the geoduck (*Panopea generosa*) is a leviathan. With two siphons that can grow to be over three feet long, this is the largest burrowing clam in the world, and it can live more than 150 years. The pronunciation of its English name ("gooey-duck") is derived from Lushootseed, an important local Native language. It is unclear why the clam's English spelling does not match its pronunciation, but correct pronunciation is a means of distinguishing those in the know. These clams are highly valuable for their meat, and accordingly some are now grown by aquaculture for the export market. Many are still harvested from the wild, however, and going after a gigantic clam with a shovel is a multihour rite of passage for some Northwesterners.

The dual three-foot-long siphons serve a purpose, of course: the clam buries itself that far underground using a powerful foot, then extends its siphons like snorkels up to the surface of the sediment, where the tips of the siphons just barely emerge from the mud. The geoduck then makes a living by sucking seawater down through its incurrent siphon, filtering out a meal of plankton, and returning the filtered water via a parallel excurrent siphon. Ensconced so far underground, it is safe from predators—including all but the most dedicated humans—and yet perfectly able to eat continuously, a feat made possible by its indiscreet-looking appendage.

Pacific Oyster

The Pacific oyster (*Crassostrea gigas*) plays a substantial role in its adopted state of Washington. These oysters were introduced from Japan in the 1920s to replace the native Olympia oyster (*Ostrea lurida*), which had been depleted by harvesting. During the California gold rush, Olympia oysters were shipped in large quantities to San Francisco, where they were a favorite food of miners—Mark Twain was one such fan—but by the end of the nineteenth century, populations had plummeted.

Now important to Washington's maritime economy, Pacific oysters are grown in the nutrient-rich waters of Willapa Bay, Grays Harbor, Hood Canal, and Puget Sound. Oysters are cultivated in racks or trays or bags or right along the muddy bottom of estuaries. As they feed, oysters filter

The Pacific oyster (*Crassostrea gigas*) is native to Japan and has invaded local shorelines in sheltered habitats. It is regularly cultivated for the seafood market.

large volumes of seawater, removing many of the phytoplankton contained in the seawater. As a consequence, oysters help maintain good water quality while also providing economic benefits to local communities. But at the same time, Pacific oysters reduce food available for native species, and oyster cultivation can occupy large swaths of estuary habitat.

Sand Dollar

Many of us first encounter sand dollars (*Dendraster excentricus*) when they're dead, their bleached-gray tests (external hard coverings) washed up on a sandy beach. When alive, they are purple and covered in what appears to be fur; this is instead many small tube feet, each an independent, hydraulically powered appendage. Beneath the waves, these creatures can reach astounding densities of up to sixty animals per square foot, mobile armies marching at odd angles through soft sediment.

In whatever manner you encounter them, sand dollars seem like they shouldn't exist—they are just so flat, so different from animals we more usually see. But they make more sense if you think of them as sea urchins that have been squashed into the shape of pancakes. And this, essentially, is what they are.

Like urchins, they have a central mouth on the underside and are covered in tube feet. Unlike urchins, sand dollars have an anus that is hidden near the outer edge, and they specialize in gleaning small food particles from water or sand. They have fine rows of tiny cilia (short hair-like structures) that form conveyor belts, transporting particles to their mouths and digestive tracts; they digest whatever they can and cast the rest out. To facilitate this sort of feeding, sand dollars anchor themselves in the sediment, leaving half of their bodies exposed to the water column. In the event that a low tide exposes them, they bury themselves to hide, leaving shoreline visitors with the mistaken impression that sand dollars are nothing more than the handful of worn gray skeletons found lying on the sand as the tide retreats.

Orange Sea Cucumber

The orange sea cucumber (*Cucumaria miniata*) is a small echinoderm (a phylum of marine animals that also includes sea stars, urchins, and sand dollars) that is easily spotted in intertidal areas along the West Coast. Its orange-red-brown body has lateral stripes of tube feet that travel the

The orange sea cucumber (*Cucumaria miniata*) pokes out from its den between rocks in the low intertidal.

length of its body. Its branching, brightly colored orange tentacles are an unmistakable identifier of this species. A close relative, *C. pallida*, also lives in these waters but is white.

Like other echinoderms, sea cucumbers have radial symmetry, with appendages occurring in multiples of five. Orange sea cucumbers have fifteen sets of feeding arms, which they use to capture small invertebrates and other organic material suspended in the water, quickly shuttling those items toward their mouth. *Cucumaria* are preyed on by sea stars, and fish will nip at their extended tentacles, so finding a good rock under which to hide is a key to their survival.

Plainfin Midshipman

Under rocks at low tide along Hood Canal, the observant visitor may find one (or many) male plainfin midshipman (*Porichthys notatus*). It is an odd-looking member of the toadfish family, and it is no ordinary fish. One might even say the midshipman is sort of a superhero of low-energy environments, with an almost-unbelievable array of quirky talents.

A fish found under a rock at low tide is quite likely a male plainfin midshipman guarding his nest of fertilized eggs. He will tend these eggs well after they hatch into juveniles, fanning them to improve their supply of oxygen and even hydrating them if they dry out (say, during an exceptionally low tide). And speaking of drying out . . . this fish can handle it, since it can breathe air and can tolerate low-oxygen conditions for significant stretches of time.

Moreover, many of these fish—although not the ones in Puget Sound—are bioluminescent during courtship, producing light from hundreds of small dots on the sides and bottoms of their bodies. The arrangement of these dots reminds some observers of the buttons on naval uniforms, hence the species' common name. The midshipman likely steals compounds necessary to produce this light from crustaceans that they eat; since these crustaceans don't live in northern waters, only more southerly fish have access to the necessary compounds.

Finally, these fish are loud. The males, in particular, make a humming sound that attracts egg-bearing females, and the males also make audible grunting noises when fighting. The sounds are loud enough to be heard on land and in some places can keep coastal residents awake at night.

So there you have it. A fish that takes care of its young, breathes air, steals crustacean molecules to help it glow in the dark, and keeps humans up all night with its humming.

Orca

Orca whales (*Orcinus orca*) can be found in all oceans, tending to prefer coastal areas and high latitudes over the open ocean. Along the US West Coast, orcas range from California to Alaska and in many places can be spotted from land.

Orcas are the largest members of the dolphin family, with notable diversity among them. Three groups of orcas appear in the region, distinguished by their behavior and diet. Resident orcas eat fish and tend to consistently return to particular places. Transient orcas roam more widely than residents and eat other marine mammals. Offshore orcas, about which less is known, inhabit waters far offshore and eat schooling fish.

Resident orcas most reliably visit the San Juan Islands. Known collectively as the Southern Resident killer whales, this group ranges from California to Alaska in winter, consistently returning to Puget Sound and the Salish Sea in spring, summer, and fall. The Southern Residents consist

The orca whale (*Orcinus orca*) is one of the region's top predators. Photo by Melissa Foley.

of three family groups, or pods. Two of these are relatively small—J pod, with about twenty-two individuals, and K pod, with about seventeen—while at about thirty-two members the third, L pod, is considerably larger. Births and deaths each year bump these numbers up or down and are big enough news that they routinely make the prime-time television and radio broadcasts in Seattle. But the overall population has declined steadily over the years and has protected status under the Endangered Species Act. The preferred prey of the Southern Residents is salmon, especially large chinook salmon, some runs of which are protected species themselves.

Resident whales have strong social structures, with lifelong family bonds organized along matrilineal lines. Orcas mingle with other pods to mate, but otherwise return to their family unit to raise their young. They can live to be quite old if the conditions are right, with some animals reaching the age of ninety years or more.

Orcas feature prominently in Pacific Northwest Indigenous cultures, often depicted in artwork and history, storytelling and cultural practices. The whales are especially visible from Lime Kiln Point State Park on the west side of San Juan Island; with luck and persistence, visitors can also spy orcas from promontories along the coasts of Washington and Oregon.

SALMON AND HUMANS IN WESTERN WASHINGTON

In the rest of the country, salmon is a food. And it is singular. In the Pacific Northwest, salmon is a universe, and it is plural. There are five species of Pacific salmon native to North America—chinook, coho, sockeye, pink, and chum—and each river may have one or more runs of each species. Each such run may be genetically distinct. And although most commercial salmon fishing happens in Alaska (not Washington), the cultural, social, and recreational fabric of the Puget Sound region is inextricably linked with this beguiling set of fishes.

Confusingly, species may go by different common names in different places, though each has its own corresponding Latin name. Chinook (*Oncorhynchus tshawytscha*) is also known as king salmon; coho (*O. kisutch*) is called silver in Canada and elsewhere; pink salmon (*O. gorbuscha*) are sometimes called humpback salmon or "humpies" for the pronounced hump on the back of reproductive males; chum salmon (*O. keta*) are also known as dog salmon, supposedly because they are not among the tastiest and therefore would be fed to dogs. Sockeye salmon (*O. nerka*) seems to be the only species known by just the one common name.

Salmon runs are a signal ecological event, an annual metronome by which the people, eagles, trees, and other living things keep time. In general, nutrients run downhill from the land into the ocean, but salmon reverse this process: in swimming upstream from the ocean to spawn and then die, salmon pump nutrients uphill from the ocean back onto the land. The result is a tight connection between land and sea, in which fish fertilize forests. Good years for ocean productivity are good years for forest productivity. As humans have come to dominate the

A sockeye salmon (*Oncorhynchus nerka*) returns to its natal stream to spawn.

landscape, the salmon have suffered in direct consequence. This has led to some degree of reckoning on the part of those same humans and an ongoing social conversation about the trade-offs between ecology and economy that may—or may not—be inherent.

The Indigenous peoples of the region have relied on salmon for spiritual and physical sustenance for millennia. The famous abundance of historical salmon runs was the cornerstone on which cultures in the region arose and flourished. In the wake of European and then American colonization, a commercial fishing and canning industry blossomed and prospered for a time before falling apart as the salmon runs dwindled. Infrastructure development, habitat loss, and pollution associated with a surge in people and economic activity took their toll. Dams, delivering reliable power and flood control, blocked access to spawning habitat, and as the twentieth century wore on, people faced the possibility of losing salmon entirely from the Salish Sea.

Hatcheries and more hatcheries failed to solve the problem. So too did fish ladders up the sides of dams, efforts to truck fish around barriers in tanker trucks, and so on.

In the context of relative scarcity, the very right to catch salmon became a civil-rights flash point, complete with state fish and game agents beating Indigenous fishermen as cameras rolled. Federal courts subsequently affirmed the existing Tribal treaty rights to harvest salmon and other natural resources, and the Western Washington US District Court has now spent decades overseeing salmon management in Washington.

Through all of this, the great runs of the past have not returned, but the fish have persisted. Various salmon runs along the West Coast are federally threatened or endangered. Some are holding steady or even increasing. Nevertheless, these fish species are at the core of many human identities in the Pacific Northwest, and the story of these remarkable fishes—and humans' relationship to them—continues to evolve.

4

n portion of Washington's outer coast is far rockier than the sandy southern portion.

WASHINGTON'S
OUTER COAST

I t sometimes feels like there's no wildness left in the world. And then there are places like the outer coast of Washington State, which strikes even the most casual visitor as a place apart: trees are many, humans are few, and the ocean tends to bash the shore with great enthusiasm. This is a destination rather than a waypoint. The Olympic Peninsula—the landmass on which the northern two-thirds of Washington's Pacific coastline sits—sticks up like the thumb of the state's closed hand, rocky shores pinched between the (geologically) young Olympic Mountains and the relentless Pacific. The coastal strip of Olympic National Park occupies much of this western seashore, forming a long, linear companion to the much-larger main body of the park occupying the interior of the Olympic Peninsula. The entirety of Olympic National Park is a UN World Heritage Site, and for good reason.

It doesn't take an expert to appreciate the biodiversity and complexity of coastal Washington. The expansive vistas and any number of beaches along US Highway 101 that encircles the Olympic Peninsula beckon travelers to stop and breathe deeply, taking in the sights and sounds. During low tides, the nooks and crannies of the rocky tidepools invite the adventurer into a different world full of stranger-than-fiction life-forms that most people rarely get to see, and this diversity of life is much of what draws visitors to the northern Washington coast.

To the south, the rocky shore gives way to a wide expanse of sand from the outflows of the Columbia River and the more moderately sized

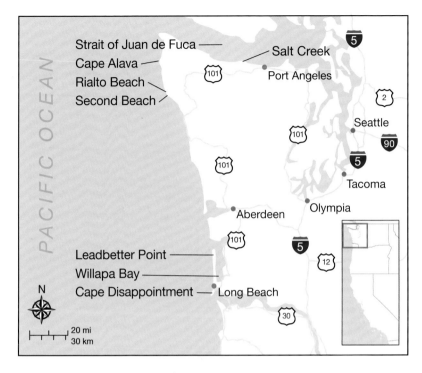

Featured locations on Washington's outer coast

rivers that create the estuaries of Grays Harbor and Willapa Bay. Here, the human population is somewhat larger—although this is not saying much, given that the biggest town is Aberdeen, with a population of about 16,000. Aberdeen and surrounding settlements grew up in the early twentieth century as the logging industry boomed, and today they still maintain an economy focused on natural resources. Just south of Willapa Bay and its Long Beach Peninsula is the mouth of the mighty Columbia, discharging freshwater sufficient to dilute the sea for miles in every direction. Astoria sits across the state line in Oregon, a picturesque reminder of a time when fur trading could fuel a regional economy.

The ecology of Washington's outer coast, as in many places, follows its landforms. The rocky northern coast hosts intertidal species suited for life on hard substrate and hardy enough to withstand strong waves.

The southern coast offers more shelter and consequently more soft-sediment habitat; species that do well here must tolerate the demanding conditions of estuaries and tend to live below the surface of mudflats or sandy beaches.

While it's always an adventure visiting Washington's outer coast, low tide puts far more marine life on display. Visiting the locations detailed in this chapter on a 0.0-foot or lower tide promises a good show. The best daytime low tides tend to be in the summer in the Pacific Northwest. There are many options for checking the tide online; a good resource is the National Oceanic and Atmospheric Administration's website.

Warning: a very low tide is coupled with a very high tide about six hours before and after. Find a way back to higher ground as the tide rises; tides can come in quickly.

PLACES TO EXPLORE ON THE ROCKY NORTHERN COAST
Strait of Juan de Fuca

Fewer than thirty minutes west of Port Angeles, on the northern edge of the Olympic Peninsula lies Salt Creek Recreation Area, with access to the Strait of Juan de Fuca shoreline. Situated midway between the inland waters of Puget Sound and the exposed outer coast, this county park offers intertidal habitats characteristic of those along the strait's southern shore. Here, salty, nutrient-rich ocean waters entering the strait from the west intermittently mix with less salty, more estuarine waters from Puget Sound, creating transitional oceanographic conditions. Wave action, too, is intermediate here, being less energetic than on the outer coast, but far more energetic than at sites within Puget Sound.

These intermediate conditions support a diverse intertidal community that includes outer-coast species living at the more protected edge of their range. Bright-green surfgrass (*Phyllospadix* spp.) is one example: surfgrass is common in wave-swept areas of the outer coast but absent from calm sites within Puget Sound. In the lower intertidal here, kelps are prominent, including *Laminaria setchelli*, which sports tough blades on stiff, woody stipes akin to the stems of land plants. Like surfgrass,

Salt Creek's broad, rocky bench—here, exposed during low tide—creates a wide intertidal zone on the Strait of Juan de Fuca that hosts an outstanding diversity of life-forms. The surfgrass (*Phyllospadix scouleri*) and subtidal kelp (*Laminaria setchellii*) at the water's edge mark the lower limit of the intertidal zone; a swath of chocolate brown denotes the diverse mid intertidal zone, with animals taking cover under many different species of algae, including the intertidal kelp called sea cabbage (*Hedophyllum sessile*); and bare rock and green and red seaweeds distinguish the higher intertidal, where species must spend more time in air than in water.

L. setchelli is common on the outer coast but absent from more protected waters. On the other hand, the sea cabbage (*Hedophyllum sessile*) tolerates a range of conditions, from wave-exposed areas of the outer coast to calmer waters typical of the San Juan Islands and Deception Pass. And rockweed (*Fucus distichus*) has an even broader tolerance for wave conditions, occurring at exposed sites on the outer coast and in protected areas throughout Puget Sound.

Invertebrates here are a similar mix of those typical of the outer coast and of inside waters. The California mussel (*Mytilus californianus*) occupies large patches at this site; this species is common on the outer

Many invertebrates, like this Pacific blood star (*Henricia leviuscula*), seek refuge under the blades of kelps—here, sea cabbage (*Hedophyllum sessile*)—to escape the afternoon sun.

coast but absent from the protected waters of Puget Sound. Dog whelks (*Nucella* spp.), the black katy chiton (*Katharina tunicata*), and the purple sea urchin (*Strongylocentrotus purpuratus*) span the range of habitats from the exposed outer coast to more protected waters.

The Wild Olympic Coast

The outer coastline of the Olympic Peninsula is almost completely within Olympic National Park, and in most cases visitors must make a short walk or a moderate day hike out to the shoreline itself.

CAPE ALAVA

A flat three-mile hike from the Lake Ozette parking area, Cape Alava can also be walked as part of a nine-mile loop: three miles through coastal forest, three miles along the beach, and another three miles back through forest. Low tide at Cape Alava reveals an expansive, low-relief rocky habitat among cobbles and boulders. Here the shore is wide and flat, so when the tide drops a few feet in the vertical dimension, it exposes tens of yards in the horizontal. The resulting intertidal zones are accordingly broader and more subtle: moving from the edge of the forest toward the waterline, the species making up the invertebrate and seaweed communities gradually change. These zones reflect microhabitats that vary ever so slightly from one another, each being favored by particular species.

Who lives where, and for how long, depends on how stable the immediate habitat is in the face of disturbance imposed by wave forces. Cobbles and smaller rocks are mobilized by wave action, especially during big storms. Moving cobbles alter the physical shape of the habitat and often crush organisms in the process. These physical disturbances can influence community structure and intertidal diversity, creating assemblages that differ from those found on rocky benches, in some cases selecting for smaller or shorter-lived species.

Despite the threat of lethal disturbance, this highly three-dimensional habitat supports a host of invertebrates capable of quick movement. In pools, small crustaceans move about, along with hermit crabs and

Low tide at Cape Alava reveals boulder and cobble fields, plenty of shallow tidepools, and lots of hiding places for invertebrates. Unlike a massive, rocky bench, cobbles and boulders shift in heavy surf, creating habitats that change constantly.

sculpins. Higher up on the beach, periwinkle snails and dog whelks are common in areas dominated by barnacles, mussels, and rockweed. Crabs are abundant here, finding refuge in the spaces between or under cobbles. Blades of seaweed offer protection from desiccation at low tide and serve as substrate for isopods (*Idotea* spp.). Isopods, relatives of terrestrial pill bugs, tend to be dorsoventrally flattened (flattened top to bottom). They tenaciously cling to their seaweed hosts using hooked claws, and the strength of their attachment seems to depend on the strength of the seaweed, not the animal—that is, some seaweed species provide better, more secure attachment than others. When motivated, these isopods can crawl or even swim to new hosts.

The lowest tides at Cape Alava reveal species that are found only in wave-exposed areas. Look especially for giant kelp (*Macrocystis pyrifera*). This is the same species that creates the iconic kelp beds of California. In Washington, giant kelp doesn't achieve the large size typical of more

A crowd of black turban snails (*Tegula funebralis*) congregates on coralline algae in a tidepool. Note the substrate of small cobbles and gravel, typical of Cape Alava and easily rearranged by wave action.

southerly regions, but it's still an impressive find. Giant kelp is restricted to Washington's outer coast and to the western reaches of the Strait of Juan de Fuca; it is absent from the calmer waters of Puget Sound, where its relative bull kelp (*Nereocystis leutkeana*) dominates (see Species of Interest in chapter 3, Washington's Puget Sound and Greater Salish Sea), and it's entirely absent from the sandy beaches to the south.

All this seaweed can make beaches here—indeed, all along the outer coast—somewhat fragrant. Masses of seaweed cast ashore by big waves become, in essence, giant compost heaps, decaying with exposure to air and producing an odor both loved and hated. Scientists who study algae (phycologists) tend to be among those who love the smell of seaweed as it rots on the beach. Some can even identify algal species based on their smell alone.

The distinctive smell of decaying seaweed on a rocky or sandy beach is due in part to bromophenols, a class of compounds containing bromine, an element related to chlorine and iodine. Those with a keen sense of smell may be able to tease out the iodine-like smells on a beach full of seaweed wrack. The ecological role of bromophenols is not entirely clear, but it's thought that they may provide defense against invertebrate grazers.

There's life beyond the tidepools at Cape Alava. Bald eagles (see Birds of the Exposed Coast in chapter 5, The Northern Oregon Coast) are regular visitors to the beach and the sea stacks, searching for an easy meal; whales pass by offshore, easily spotted by their misty spouts, and harbor seals (see Marine Mammals in chapter 6, The Southern Oregon Coast) rest on rocks just above the water's reach. Even sea otters are here; indeed, this is one of the only spots in Washington or Oregon where sea otters have successfully been reintroduced after their extirpation by fur traders.

RIALTO BEACH

Near the center of the coastal strip of Olympic National Park, Rialto Beach lies just north of La Push. Here, the beach is exposed to the full force of winter storms without the protection of a broad, flat bench, as at Cape Alava. The narrow, steep beach at Rialto is covered with coarse sand, small cobbles, and logs. Storm-generated winter waves cause so

Differential rates of erosion cause striations in this sedimentary rock at Rialto Beach. A few hardy species find purchase in the depressions.

much movement of the substrate that most organisms simply aren't able to withstand the disturbance—they are crushed or covered by sand. Consequently, there is relatively little marine life among the sand and cobbles nearest the parking lot. But a walk to the far end of the beach, well north of the parking lot, reveals a low rocky bench that hosts patches of the most tenacious mussels, barnacles, and seaweeds, which in turn harbor a suite of motile invertebrates (those capable of some form of movement).

About a mile from the parking lot sits Hole-in-the-Wall, a natural stone arch through which visitors can walk. Over time, erosion of the relatively soft sedimentary rock has created an intertidal landscape of varying appearance: smooth, rounded substrates punctuated by small pools give way to flat benches marked with long rocky stripes reflecting the geological processes that formed these benches. Biological cover can be sparse on these sedimentary surfaces, especially in winter. Some areas harbor dense patches of invertebrates, including California mussels (*Mytilus californianus*) and periwinkle snails (*Littorina* spp.), and the

Hole-in-the-Wall, a favorite destination on the Washington coast, is a sea stack in the making: waves have eroded softer rock, leaving a more durable column behind.

Periwinkles (*Littorina* spp.) are marine snails that can survive out of the water for extended periods of time. They're often found in dense aggregations in rocky intertidal areas.

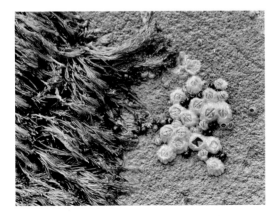

Moving up and down the shore with the tides, periwinkles (*Littorina* spp.) hide in the nooks and crannies created by barnacles (center) and use nearby seaweeds (left) as a place to forage. The scale here is small: the barnacle patch is only about two inches across.

nearly vertical walls of some of the rocky features here offer excellent examples of intertidal zonation (see chapter 2, Living between the Tides).

SECOND BEACH

A short walk of little over a mile leads from a parking area to Second Beach, where towering sea stacks provide habitat for hundreds of nesting seabirds, including tufted puffins (*Fratercula cirrhata*; see Birds of the Exposed Coast in chapter 5, The Northern Oregon Coast), which are rare in the continental US, and marbled murrelets (*Brachyramphus marmoratus*), listed under the US Endangered Species Act.

At their base, the headlands create rocky intertidal habitat that can be accessible on a low tide. Urchins, hermit crabs, snails, sea stars, barnacles, mussels, and fish all are here. In this crowded place, the sea stars and chitons and limpets play important roles by clearing space on the rocks for new occupants. Massive assemblages of California mussels (*Mytilus*

Second Beach offers beautiful and easily accessible intertidal habitat, especially during summer months. Sea stacks—geologic remnants that formerly were connected to the mainland—sit just offshore, and at low tide it's possible to walk out to the stacks closest to shore.

This aggregating anemone (*Anthopleura elegantissima*) has bright, translucent pink-tipped tentacles; others of the same species house photosynthetic algae in their tissues, which turn the host animal green. This clonal species often grows in patches, hence its common name; each aggregation is a clone of a genetically distinct individual, and the aggregations are produced through repeated fission—that is, division of an individual polyp.

californianus) and gooseneck barnacles (*Pollicipes polymerus*) dominate areas of rock higher up, crowding out other species and advertising the wave-swept conditions.

Drift logs are part of this dynamic scene and have been for as long as there have been big trees, delivered to the shore by rivers that drain the nearby Olympic Mountains. Once in the ocean, drift logs are transported on currents and lifted by waves, often returning to shore in a highly energetic fashion, crushing intertidal organisms where they land and opening space in an otherwise crowded landscape. The disturbance created by drift logs is a major force structuring intertidal communities in the Pacific Northwest.

For example, patches of mussels can completely cover the rocks in this region, excluding other would-be occupants. But just as a large tree falling in a forest opens up space that is readily colonized by other species, a drift

The byssal threads of the California mussel (*Mytilus californianus*) create strong attachments to the substrate. The threads are made primarily of collagen proteins and don't contain living cells—they can be discarded and regrown over time.

log can dislodge mussels, allowing other species to move in, at least temporarily. Here, visitors may be able to detect mussel patches of differing ages, some dominated by large older individuals and others by smaller younger individuals.

Drift logs play another important role in the beach ecosystem, but with a more terrestrial connection. Large black carpenter ants inhabit these giant woodpiles, excavating tunnels that network nests in the logs to house their young. Unlike termites, however, carpenter ants eat dead insects rather than the wood itself.

The ants illustrate a larger point about the coastal zone: where the sea meets the land, exchanges of food and energy go both ways. It isn't merely fish that forage in the sand when the tide is high but also insects, feeding and laying eggs in kelp rafts or transient pools, and birds, pecking in the sand or swooping in from the sky to find a meal. Land and sea are tightly intertwined in coastal food webs.

SPECIES OF INTEREST ON THE ROCKY NORTHERN COAST

Rockweed

Rockweed (*Fucus distichus*) is a common brown alga often associated with lower-energy environments throughout the northern hemisphere, although it can also occasionally live on some wave-swept shores. It tolerates an impressive array of conditions, being equally happy in brackish water and full salt water, and it can even survive freezing during exposure on cold low tides. Like many other red and brown seaweeds, rockweed harbors chemical compounds that deter would-be predators from chowing down on their tissues. *Fucus distichus* has a branching shape, and at the end of each branch a bladder develops with age. The bladder is filled with air, helping the fronds to remain upright in the water column when the tide is up, maximizing their exposure to sunlight. Reproductive structures develop on the bladders, appearing as small raised bumps that release eggs and sperm when the time is right.

Like many seaweeds, rockweed provides valuable cover at low tide to many invertebrate species that would otherwise dry out in a sunny,

Rockweed (*Fucus distichus)* is among the most common species on high intertidal shores.

waterless environment. *Fucus distichus* itself readily dries out when exposed during warm low tides, only to be rehydrated by the oncoming tide hours later.

Big Trees

The Pacific Northwest owes much of its identity and history to its trees. Western Washington and Oregon host the densest temperate forests on the planet, a congregation of conifers that thoroughly dominates the landscape, fueled by persistent winter rains and summer sun and shaped over geological time. All four of the tree species described below are among the largest conifers in the world. And individual trees of all four species can live for hundreds of years, longer than the vast majority of human governments in world history.

Apart from defining the look and feel of coastal Pacific Northwest, these trees are the context in which the region's coastal ecology plays out. Witness, for example, the great rain-forest trees of the Olympic Peninsula that, downstream among the tidepools, become driftwood battering rams. The forest's birds and mammals emerge to hunt among the waves and boulders, key predators in intertidal food webs. And salmon deliver ocean nutrients upstream, feeding the giant stands of western red cedar, Douglas fir, Sitka spruce, and western hemlock. This mix of coastal species delineates Washington and Oregon from northern California, where the coast redwood (*Sequoia sempervirens*) and associated species become dominant.

WESTERN RED CEDAR

The imposingly dignified western red cedar (*Thuja plicata*) has long furnished coastal Indigenous communities with the materials for many of life's activities: wood for housing, boatbuilding, ceremonial poles, and utensils; roots and bark for clothing, rope, and baskets, and so on.

DOUGLAS FIR

Douglas fir (*Pseudotsuga menziesii*), home to the northern spotted owl and the red tree vole, among many other forest species, is one of the most important timber trees in the world.

SITKA SPRUCE

The beautiful and strong Sitka spruce (*Picea sitchensis*) hugs the coastline; its wood kept the Wright brothers aloft and supported the early aircraft industry in Seattle, and it continues to grace musical instruments worldwide.

WESTERN HEMLOCK

The shade-tolerant western hemlock (*Tsuga heterophylla*) often grows on the vestiges of its fallen neighbors in damp coastal forests; like the red cedar, it can live for many centuries.

Black Katy Chiton

Scores of black katy chitons (*Katharina tunicata*) cling to the rocks at Pacific Northwest sites exposed to intense wave action. They often associate with pink coralline algae, a colorful contrast to the chiton's dark form. Characterized by their dark color and diamond-shaped cream-colored patches of visible shell, these molluscs make their living like most other chitons: by slowly cruising along the rocks, scraping up algae as they go.

Black katy chitons (*Katharina tunicata)* are distinguishable by the leather-like mantle that surrounds the calcareous plates.

Because they are formidable grazers, katy chitons strongly influence the species of kelps and other algae that can live nearby.

The katy chiton can grow up to about five inches in length, large enough that it has been an important food source for local Indigenous communities historically—and in some cases, it is still eaten, especially in British Columbia and Alaska. Consumed either raw or cooked, chitons have been a reliable and substantial part of traditional diets.

Leather Limpet

One of the more charming invertebrates on rocky shores is sometimes known as the leather limpet (*Onchidella borealis*), despite its not being a limpet. This species is instead a marine slug—that is, a snail without a shell—that has a somewhat leathery covering. It's small, typically less than a half inch in length, and often reddish or brownish in color with a distinctive scalloped edge.

It tends to live in the mid to high intertidal zone among red algae, roaming lower on the shore to feed during low tide, then returning "home" as the tide rises. Why is this little slug so attuned to the tides? Different from most sea slugs, *Onchidella* has lungs and breathes air, so it prefers to stay high and dry when the tide is up. And those scalloped

The leather limpet (*Onchidella borealis*) is, in fact, not a limpet at all but, rather, an air-breathing small sea slug. Photo by Alyssa Gehman.

edges secrete a fluid that repels predators like the small six-armed star (*Leptasterias hexactis*).

Shore Crabs

Quick small crustaceans, shore crabs inevitably scatter from underneath overturned rocks. They stare out from cracks between high intertidal boulders, hiding until nightfall, when they are most active. In general, these crabs are well adapted to life in air, equipped with reduced gills that leave them better able to breathe out of the water than in it. They are the scavengers of the shore, eating primarily sea lettuce (*Ulva* spp.) and other algae but happy to take meals wherever they might be found.

Three species of shore crabs are common in the Pacific Northwest. The purple shore crab (*Hemigrapsus nudus*), most common on exposed rocky shores, has a red-purple carapace and conspicuous purple spots on its claws. Its close relative *H. oregonensis* is somewhat more likely to be found in quieter, more protected areas; it is grayish green, without spots, and has notably hairy walking legs. The third species, the lined shore crab (*Pachygrapsus crassipes*), is common only in southern Oregon and south

The purple shore crab (*Hemigrapsus nudus*) is one of three common shore crab species along the West Coast. The telltale sign it's a purple crab is its spotted claws, which are used for defense and for foraging.

to Baja California. Although its color can vary from green to red to black, it has conspicuous lines across its carapace, hence its common name.

Hermit Crabs

A tidepool observer will soon realize that many of the small shells in pools are moving in un-snail-like ways, as several different species of the hermit crab genus (*Pagurus*) wander about. Opportunistic shell dwellers, these tiny crabs find discarded snail shells (or sometimes clam or other shells) to carry on their backs as mobile homes, protecting their soft bodies from predation. Famously, when they outgrow the shell they have, they drop it and find another, bigger shell to inhabit; by observing long enough, you might witness crabs battling over a newly available shell that is just the right size.

Some species of hermit crab have preferences for the shells of particular snail species: for instance, *Pagurus samuelis* tends to prefer the shells of black turban snails (*Tegula* spp.). Other species of hermit crab in this region

Hermit crabs (*Pagurus* spp.) live in abandoned shells, in this case the shell of the snail *Nucella*.

favor the shells of dog whelks (*Nucella* spp.), dire whelks (*Lirabuccinum* spp.), and periwinkle snails (*Littorina* spp.). Hermit crabs make their living by feeding on seaweeds, microalgae, and detritus (dead organic matter). These small crabs are full of character, some shy, some bold.

Gooseneck Barnacles

The strange-looking, stalked creatures on coasts that have lots of wave action are a species of gooseneck barnacle (*Pollicipes polymerus*). If you squint a bit, they bear a passing resemblance to the neck and head of a goose—or at least enough of a resemblance that it led to centuries of European mythology surrounding them. The story, it seems, went like this: not understanding the migratory patterns of geese in northern Europe, people were at a loss to explain how they hadn't ever seen baby geese, yet the birds showed up each year, fully grown. The gooseneck barnacle was thought to be the fruit of a kind of barnacle tree and, when mature, would (somehow) turn into a grown bird. And cleverly, some Catholic clergy saw this as a way to allow eating meat on days when doing so was otherwise

These gooseneck barnacles (*Pollicipes polymerus*) grow in dense clumps in areas exposed to waves and surge. They grow slowly and can live for two decades.

forbidden: according to legend, the goose hadn't been born in the usual way, so it didn't count as meat.

Obviously, none of this mythology reflects real biology. But the actual facts of the gooseneck barnacle are nevertheless intriguing. Like other barnacles, these feed with their feet, plucking small particles out of the plankton. But unlike more standard barnacles, these don't do the work of moving their feeding appendages around; instead, they rely on the motion of the water to do that for them. They are therefore restricted to high-energy environments in which they can safely wait for their food to come to them.

A very close look at a clump of gooseneck barnacles reveals a cryptic form of a limpet (*Lottia digitalis*) living on the barnacle's calcareous plates. This form of *L. digitalis* typically produces a white or light-colored shell sporting a number of dark stripes that resemble the dark sutures between the calcareous plates of the barnacle. These cryptic limpets can be very difficult to discern, at least for the human eye. Birds, too, may have a tough time finding cryptic limpets living on gooseneck barnacles, and avoiding predators may be one advantage of this cryptic coloration.

A different species of gooseneck barnacle (*Lepas anatifera*) whose Latin name reflects its European goose mythology occasionally shows up on beached driftwood and other structures along the US West Coast. It isn't an intertidal species but, rather, one that lives worldwide out at sea, attached to anything that floats. Seeing it on the beach is a treat, inspiring thoughts of the oceanic voyages that the species undertakes, all as a passenger with no control over its destination.

Ochre Sea Star

If tomorrow an alien landed in our midst from a distant world, it couldn't be a much stranger life-form than a sea star. And yet here they are: not symmetrical in the left-right way we usually think of, but instead organized radially around a central disc. With bodies that, thanks to connective tissue that can form and break collagen bonds, can be rigid one second and floppy the next. With both circulatory and muscular systems that are hydraulic, running on seawater. With thousands of sucking

Common on many Pacific Northwest rocky shores, the ochre sea star (*Pisaster ochraceus*) strongly influences the structure of intertidal communities.

tube feet that hold and release using the same hydraulic mechanism, able to withstand the heaviest of wave action. With arms they can excise and regenerate at will. With special sensory feet at the end of each arm. With tiny pincers all over their bodies that grab and remove particles or would-be parasites. With stomachs that digest food outside of the body rather than in the customary way. And without a brain, but instead with radial nerves and a nerve net complex enough to make sea stars one of the most formidable predators along the shore.

These seemingly alien creatures move among us. Their cousins—sea urchins, sand dollars, and sea cucumbers—too, can be deeply weird: for example, sea cucumbers that breathe through their anus or eviscerate themselves through pores in their body walls, or purple sea urchins that produce teeth strong enough to burrow into steel pilings.

Along much of the rocky outer coast of North America, the ochre sea star (*Pisaster ochraceus*) often draws a lot of attention as beachgoers browse among the rocks. Though they're often bright orange or vibrant purple, some are a duller brownish-purple. All are the same species, and the different color morphs are, to date, ecologically indistinguishable.

The ochre sea star is the original example of a keystone species in the intertidal zone. Their keystone role is attributable to their ability to transform intertidal communities. Ochre sea stars prey on dense groupings of California mussels (*Mytilus californianus*), which in the absence of ochre sea stars can completely cover hard surfaces, excluding other species and thereby changing the diversity along the shore. Where ochre sea stars are numerous, their voracious feeding removes mussels and opens space for other species to move in, changing the suite of species present. The recognition that one species can so strongly influence the others living around it is an important piece of the explanation for what lives where on the shore, and why.

PLACES TO EXPLORE ON THE SANDIER SOUTHERN COAST

In Washington State, parts of the beach are a highway. In the early 1900s, Washington and Oregon both declared state beaches to be highways, vesting control of these areas in the states' departments of transportation. Cars drive on these beaches today. Such driving is possible here because, unlike the northern coast of Washington, the southern coast is characterized by long, flat, sandy beaches backed by low-lying dunes and tall grasses.

But a short distance inland is another dominant ecosystem: the muddy shorelines and expansive, shallow, but productive waters of some of the West Coast's prominent estuaries. These estuaries originated as drowned river valleys formed as sea level rose after the last ice age, more recently modified by the addition of ocean-built sandbars at their entrances. Fed by rivers on their east side and ocean water on their west side, Willapa Bay and Grays Harbor teem with life where salt and freshwater mix.

Willapa Bay

The Long Beach Peninsula separates the Pacific Ocean from Willapa Bay, helping to create one of the largest estuaries on the West Coast. Although they might appear muddy and a bit less appealing than rocky shores, estuaries like Willapa Bay are in fact full of life and play a critical role in nearshore ecology. Many animals depend on estuaries as feeding grounds, places to breed, and nurseries where young fish and invertebrates like Dungeness crab can grow and hide from predators. Estuaries are also important stopover grounds for migrating birds, offering both food and rest. Oysters and clams thrive in these plankton-rich waters, and indeed Willapa Bay is an important area for commercial oyster production.

Ocean processes largely drive the productivity of Willapa Bay, illustrating a mechanism that is common to estuaries along the coast. Coastal upwelling transports nutrients from deeper waters toward the surface, and this nutrient-rich ocean water is drawn into Willapa Bay by the action of strong tides, especially during the summer. Carried along in this ocean water are the larvae of crabs, oysters, and other species that use the bay as nursery grounds. Water from the Columbia River plume at times moves northward and curls into the bay. By contrast, the more modest rivers that empty directly into Willapa Bay tend to be highly seasonal, with not much influence in summer.

Long channels, which allow salt water and freshwater to mix around the edges of Willapa Bay, have characteristic fine sediments that create a home for mud-loving animals that can tolerate fluctuations of salinity due to the inputs of both freshwater and salt water.

The plants here are true plants, as opposed to the seaweeds of the outer coast. Typically, the plants that occupy estuaries like Willapa Bay are rooted in the deep muddy or sandy sediments that cover the bottom of the bay. These rooted plants—native seagrasses and salt grasses (and some invasive cordgrasses)—are close relatives of plants that live on dry land. Seaweeds, on the other hand, lack roots and are only distantly related to land plants (see Plant, Alga, Seaweed, Kelp: Which Is It? below). The seaweeds of Willapa Bay—for example, the bright-green sea lettuce (see Species of Interest in chapter 3, Washington's Puget Sound and Greater Salish Sea)—tend to have thin blades and lack the robust structure that is common to kelps found on the outer coast. Look closely and you'll find tiny blades of seaweed growing on the leaves of seagrass. In this case, the seagrass leaves offer a firm platform for attachment among the mud and sand of the estuary.

PLANT, ALGA, SEAWEED, KELP: WHICH IS IT?

We're all familiar with plants on land. They are nearly universally green; they have leaves of some sort to capture sunlight, roots through which they take up nutrients, and often flowers by which they produce seeds. Plants occur in the intertidal zone too, but they are restricted to a small number of species. Seagrasses, including eelgrasses, are a form of true plant, and at the right time of year, close observation yields a glimpse of very cryptic flowers. Marsh plants too are true plants.

The term algae (singular alga) refers to a diverse group of unrelated taxa that tend to live in marine and aquatic environments. The green algae (e.g., sea lettuce, *Ulva* spp.) are close ancestors of true plants, but others (red algae, brown algae) are not. Like plants, algae typically are photosynthetic, but they lack many of the structures found in true plants, including roots and flowers.

A beach-cast specimen of kelp is attached by its holdfast
to the small rock that had anchored it in deeper water.

Algae can be single-celled and microscopic, or they can be multi-cellular and very large. Multicellular forms are often referred to as seaweeds: that is, seaweeds are simply many-celled large algae. With only a few exceptions, seaweeds are anchored to the substrate by holdfasts, root-like masses for attachment (remember, seaweeds have no true roots). Seaweeds use their blades to take up nutrients directly from the surrounding seawater.

Kelps are a special group of seaweeds. They belong to a single order (the Laminariales) in the brown algae, and kelps are among the largest of any of the seaweeds. Some kelps form extensive underwater forests, while others grow in intertidal areas, typically low on the shore.

Confusingly, the term *plant* is often used as shorthand for any of the large photosynthetic organisms along the shore. Hence, seaweeds are often casually referred to as plants even though they are not plants at all. And although we have tried to be precise in our writing, we too sometimes fall into this casual but imprecise terminology.

The 15,000-acre Willapa Bay National Wildlife Refuge, consisting of several sites around the bay, showcases the diverse habitats here. Each of these highlights a different element of the regional ecosystem, including tidal mudflats, sandy beaches, temperate rain forest, and freshwater streams and rivers competing to shape the coastal zone. It also includes several rare remnants of old-growth coastal red-cedar forest, and depending on the time of year, visitors might see river otters, migrating salmon and bird species, elk, and amphibians.

Leadbetter Point

At the northern tip of the Long Beach Peninsula is Leadbetter Point, a place where the estuary and ocean come together. Sandy beaches face west toward the open ocean; muddy shorelines and salt marshes face east across the large estuary. Low-lying coastal forest separates the two, occupying former dunes, with trails that run through classic coastal

The Bay Trail of Leadbetter Point State Park leads through a classic coastal forest ecosystem to the east-facing shore, whose expansive mudflats are fully exposed on the low tide.

The western snowy plover (*Charadrius nivosus*), a protected species, uses the dunes on the Long Beach Peninsula as habitat. Photo by Melissa Foley.

ecosystems dominated by spruce, huckleberry, salal, and low-lying herbs. Most of the point is protected as Leadbetter Point State Park.

The tip of the peninsula features bird-watching in all seasons, and it lies within the Willapa Bay National Wildlife Refuge. Between March and September, lucky visitors can see western snowy plovers (*Charadrius nivosus*) and their newly hatched chicks. These imperiled birds are listed as threatened under the US Endangered Species Act; they tend to nest and forage in low-lying beach habitats, and the Long Beach Peninsula fits the bill. A small shorebird about six inches long, mostly white with black patches above the forehead and behind the eye, the plovers scurry along the beach, searching for a meal of invertebrates and insects among the beach-cast kelp. Portions of the beaches are closed during the nesting season to protect the birds and their young. Visitors can view plovers from a safe distance away.

Long Beach and Cape Disappointment

Running nearly thirty miles from north to south, the west side of the Long Beach Peninsula is a very long beach. The peninsula rises just a few feet above the ocean's surface, making it particularly susceptible to sea-level

The long sandy beach of the Long Beach Peninsula ends at the rocky headland of Cape Disappointment.

rise and tsunamis. Long Beach offers little in the way of hard substrate, characterized mostly by shifting sands, except for the very southern end of the peninsula at the rockier Cape Disappointment, at the mouth of the Columbia River.

Sandy beaches dominate the intertidal in the Long Beach area, forming a highly dynamic environment in which the substrate itself is constantly shifting among waves and tides. Trillions of tiny grains of sand are constantly in motion, which means there's nothing to attach to for seaweeds or animals. Environments like this favor those that are adapted to surroundings that change quickly. Despite their seemingly low diversity, sandy beaches host a number of interesting species.

Sand crabs, also known as mole crabs (*Emerita analoga*—see Species of Interest in chapter 5, The Northern Oregon Coast), ride shallow waves that dissolve onto sandy shores. When the water recedes, the small barrel-shaped crabs burrow quickly in the sand, extending their antennae to filter plankton in the water. Following the tide up and down the beach,

SAND

One of the amazing things about the living world is that the closer we look, the more there is to see. Just as rain forests have plants growing on plants growing on plants and life exploding from every pore, so too do tidepools and beaches and rocks along the shore. Tiny sea slugs live on minute encrustations on the surface of kelp blades. Small worms live in the guts of sea cucumbers or in the grooves along the underside of a sea star's arms. Parasitic barnacles take over crabs' brains as if commandeering a passenger van. And although whole universes of creatures without common names occupy the spaces between grains of sand on a beach, in terms of obvious and interesting wildlife, sand pales in comparison to rocky shoreline habitat. Why should this be? Why should sand be so much less obviously diverse than rocks a short distance away?

In a word: stability. Most species large enough to be seen require some sort of stable, three-dimensional structure on which to make a home. Easy examples are barnacles (with shells cemented to a rock or other hard surface), kelp (with a holdfast attached to some hard surface), and limpets (grazing along rocks, needing a surface to hold on to), but really it's just about every shoreline species we could name. Any stable three-dimensional structure—such as rocks, plants, or hard parts of other species—seems to attract marine life, offering substrate and hiding places for all kinds of creatures.

Sand is sort of the opposite of a stable structure. At large spatial scales, it moves around: today's beach sand will be on a different beach next year. And at smaller spatial scales, there's nothing to hold on to. Sand slips through your fingers if you're a human just as it does through the claws of a hermit crab.

A species can mix sand with some mucus and make durable structures—some tube worms do this, for example—but moving waves of sand quickly bury tubes and burrows in the surf zone. And the coarser the sand grains, the steeper the beach tends to be, which creates a set of interconnected variables with a strong influence on which species can live where (see Sand Becomes Habitat in chapter 2, Living between the Tides).

Thus, so many of the larger-bodied species that do well in sandy habitats—such as those in chapter 6, The Southern Oregon Coast—are vagabonds, adventuring through a sandy world that is forever changing around them. Some snails and a host of small worms and crustaceans do reasonably well in these types of locales.

However, another answer to sand's challenges is to be really small. Such complexity rewards those curious enough to take a closer look. While (almost) no one goes to the beach with a microscope in hand, a careful glance with the naked eye can reveal a lot that is ordinarily too small to be noticed. Very small-bodied animals can fit easily between grains of sand, oblivious to the constant shifting going on at larger scales. And in this microscopic world, a sandy beach is a zoo of crazy-looking animals that most visitors have likely never heard of. These each compete, fight, mate, and so on, all on a tiny scale. Some commute up and down the beach with the tides, unseen, because they do so among the sand grains themselves.

each animal can change its position and has no problem surviving the crashing surf because of its armor-like hard exoskeleton.

Rather than tumbling in the surf like a sand crab, the razor clam (*Siliqua patula*) uses a different strategy to survive, digging deep in the sand to find the most secure place possible. Using a muscular foot, the clam

The siphon of a razor clam (*Siliqua patula*) pokes out of the sand on a receding tide. Eaten by Dungeness crabs, flatfish, and humans, razor clams can dig rapidly when disturbed.

buries itself and then extends its siphon to the sand's surface, where it can draw in seawater and extract small food particles from the water column above. Shells of expired razor clams often litter the beach.

Birds, too, use these sandy habitats, offering evidence of productivity that is difficult for casual observers to see. Shorebirds feeding near the water's edge hunt for small invertebrates such as beach hoppers living in the sand. Equally interesting are crows that feed high on the shore–these birds leave conspicuous holes where they have probed for larger-bodied invertebrates.

At the southernmost end of the Long Beach Peninsula stands Cape Disappointment, now a state park of the same name. John Meares, a British fur trader, gave this bit of rock its English name (it was known locally as Kah'eese), having been disappointed during his voyage south from British Columbia in 1788. The mix of freshwater, salt water, and sediment at the river mouth causes a tall and dangerous set of standing waves, which, remarkably, hide the mouth from view of passing mariners. Trying but failing to find the rumored Columbia River's mouth, Meares turned his ship back northward, conferring the place name that matched his mood.

The headland at the cape rises nearly 700 feet from the sea and is topped by a historical lighthouse. Built in 1856, the lighthouse remains a critical aid to navigation in a region that is among the foggiest in the US. The cape itself sits just barely inside the mouth of the Columbia River, facing south. Apart from being a major geographical landmark—the opening to the Pacific Northwest's biggest river, which delivers the most water to the North American part of the Pacific Ocean—it's a historical one: this is where Lewis and Clark's US Corps of Volunteers for Northwest Discovery finally reached the sea, and there is accordingly an interpretive center on the site.

Just around the cape to the north and facing west, North Head is an isolated headland surrounded by sandy beach. The headland offers space for the most robust species to attach. Barnacles are abundant in the high intertidal zone, and mussels can be found growing just a bit lower on the shore. Missing from this headland are most of the fleshy seaweeds that are typical of rocky shores to the north. Also missing or rare are many of the mobile animals, such as periwinkle snails and crabs, that are common at more northerly sites. Their absence is due to a combination of factors: the rock face here is nearly vertical, making it tough to hang on; wave action is fierce; sand scour is chronic, scraping off anything that lands on the rock; and the Columbia River pumps out an average of 265,000 cubic feet of freshwater per second, diluting the salt water past the tolerances of many marine species.

SPECIES OF INTEREST ON THE SANDIER SOUTHERN COAST

Dune Grass

Backing much of the shoreline along the Long Beach Peninsula is dune grass (*Elymus mollis*), a flowering plant and a wild relative of wheat that grows directly in sand. Dune grass stabilizes the ever-shifting sands and, by doing so, also helps build new dunes. This habitat is important for shorebirds, especially the threatened western snowy plover (*Charadrius nivosus*), which often situates a nest near a clump of dune grass.

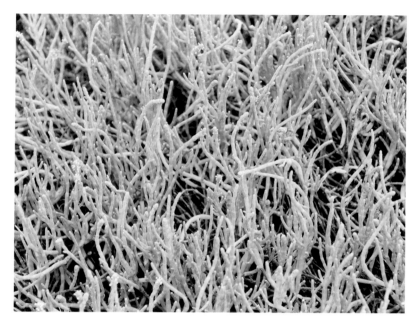
Pickleweed (*Salicornia* sp. *virginica*) can look like a grassy meadow to the casual observer.

Pickleweed

Along the mudflats of Willapa Bay and elsewhere in protected estuarine habitats grow what look like meadows of green grass. In fact it's pickleweed (*Salicornia virginica*), a salt-tolerant plant that dominates estuaries along both coasts of the continental US. Pickleweed stores salt in the plant's tips; when that gets to be too much, the tips turn red and fall off, shedding excess salt. Even though most animals do not feed on pickleweed, it's nevertheless an important plant to intertidal ecology: it stabilizes muddy sediments; numerous bird species use it for nesting; small mammals use it to seek cover. Humans use pickleweed too—in the summer, when its new growth yields tender green tips, people harvest them to use in salads, either raw or steamed.

Pickleweed can host dodder (*Cuscuta californica*), a parasitic vine that looks like nothing so much as a tangle of orange spaghetti. Dodder is almost entirely stem—hence the resemblance to noodles—and has tiny white flowers in summer, betraying its identity as a flowering plant.

A tiny beach hopper casts a long shadow on Washington's sandy southern coast.

Beach Hoppers

Beach hoppers (family Talitridae), also called simply hoppers or sand fleas (even though they aren't fleas), are found worldwide on temperate sandy beaches, including those of Washington and Oregon. Hoppers are bean-shaped small crustaceans, members of a larger group called amphipods. They typically occur in large numbers—where there is one, there are many, many more. And true to their name, they are great at hopping.

Hoppers live on sandy beaches, preferring wet sand because they are prone to dehydration. During the day they remain burrowed in damp sand high on the beach or hidden under shelter such as driftwood. Hoppers eat at night, taking advantage of more humid conditions. They typically feed on seaweed washed ashore and on detritus, using their sense of smell to find their food. Although they are a marine animal, hoppers breathe air and will drown if submerged for long periods. Fish, birds, and terrestrial predators all eat them, so they're another important link between the food webs of the sea and land. Look for them early in the morning or late in the day among clumps of decaying seaweed and under driftwood logs.

Sea stars and anemones make up a typical tidepool scene.

A large crab seeks partial refuge under a cluster of anemones.

The northern Oregon coast features long sandy beaches broken abruptly by rocky headlands.

THE
NORTHERN
OREGON
COAST

From north to south, the Oregon coast is nearly 350 miles of ocean bliss. Rocky headlands poke out into the sea, flanked by sandy beaches and extensive dunes, rivers, and estuaries that create briny ecosystems rich with species. Seaside towns range from quaint and quiet to industrial and bustling, where fishing and a maritime economy remain very much alive. The Oregon Coast Range and Siskiyou Mountains frame this coastal setting, separating the seaside towns and countryside from the economic and political centers that lie inland along Interstate 5 and lending a sense of being off the beaten path.

The state's coastline is nearly linear, facing the uninterrupted Pacific across thousands of miles to Japan and Russia. Such an unbroken stretch of water and wind gives rise to waves so powerful they are measurable on a seismometer at Corvallis, sixty miles inland. All told, the Oregon coast is one of the world's highest wave-energy environments, with larger waves in winter followed by calmer conditions in the summer. As elsewhere, the beaches here erode with winter's heavy wave action and build back up again during the summer months.

The Oregon coast predominantly consists of sandy beaches interrupted by rocky headlands, instead of the other way around, and these headlands prevent the sand from moving freely between beaches. Sand, in general, is a dominant theme all along the Oregon coast, strongly influencing what lives where, in many places favoring sand-tolerant species over others. Urchins, for example, don't tolerate sand well, and they are accordingly rare among many of the headlands here. Sea stars and anemones fare far better.

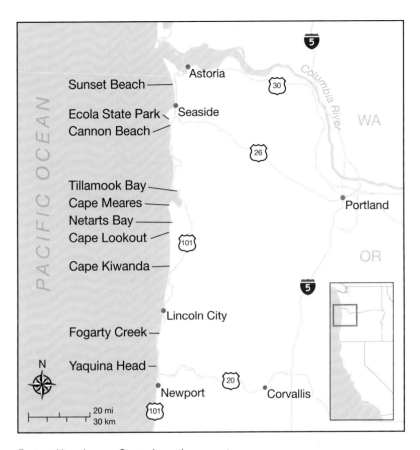

Featured locations on Oregon's northern coast

Northern Oregon begins where southern Washington leaves off: with a long stretch of sand delivered by the Columbia River. Ignoring the political boundary that delineates the two states, a single beach complex straddles the Columbia, with similar coastal ecology on each side of the river. On the Oregon side, Sunset Beach runs nearly twenty miles from the mouth of the Columbia to the northernmost headland, Tillamook Head.

The Columbia River fills the extensive beach north of Tillamook Head with angular new sand grains; beaches south of the head have older, more rounded sand grains, the product of local rivers. For example, the fine grains of Cannon Beach, worn round over time, squeak as you walk on

BEACH ACCESS AND THE PUBLIC TRUST DOCTRINE

Shorelines have an open, public quality to them. Visitors spend time at the water's edge, even when they don't own the waterfront property. Many beaches are public parks of some kind, but interestingly, many states recognize a right to access the shore even if it appears to be on private property.

This public-ness is a legal distinction that stretches back beyond the Magna Carta to Roman law (and perhaps earlier). These ancient legal authorities recognized some things common to all humankind, including the air, running water, sea, and shores. The present version of this idea comes down to us in the US as the Public Trust Doctrine: that each state holds some land and waters in trust for the benefit of its citizens. The rights to use and enjoy these places can't be sold off or privatized, and hence people are allowed to paddle along the shore or wade in the water, even if they don't own the property itself.

Washington and Oregon both recognize some version of these use and access rights. Washington courts will protect the public right to navigation, boating, swimming, fishing, and related uses of the state waters. Both the wet and dry areas of ocean beaches in Washington are customarily open to the public, although it is less clear that this applies to beaches within Puget Sound. Shoreline visitors do not appear to have a legal right to cross private property in order to access shorelines.

Oregon's state Beach Bill (1967) guarantees "free and uninterrupted use of the beaches," a strikingly broad protection for the public to use the dry-sand beaches along the entirety of Oregon's 362-mile coastline. Wet sand historically falls into the category of public-trust resources and so is public in any case. Oregon therefore has a very accessible coastline, although as in Washington, the public right to use the shoreline does not include a right to cross private property to access that shoreline.

the wide, flat expanse of sand; a walk on the beach at Seaside, just north of the head, makes no such sound.

North of Newport, nearly all of the rocky coastal outcroppings are volcanic in origin, the remnants of lava flows extinguished by the sea more than ten million years ago. Low-lying areas are made of softer younger sedimentary rock.

PLACES TO EXPLORE
Tillamook Head Area

Sitka spruce and hemlock dominate the coastal forests south of the nearly twenty-mile-long Sunset Beach, beginning at Tillamook Head, with shore pines (*Pinus contorta*) growing right on the beach in many areas. The beach-dwelling form of these pines is short and gnarled, its shape quite different from the mountain form of the same species, which grows so straight and tall that it is called the lodgepole pine.

Tillamook Head itself divides Seaside (north of the head) from Cannon Beach (south of the head), and it is the site of the first substantial rocky intertidal habitat south the central Washington coast, a distance of about a hundred miles. The head's chunk of volcanic rock occupies the Columbia's former riverbed, where lava hit the sea and cooled.

Ecola State Park, which occupies most of the headland, features a mosaic of intertidal habitats, with broad sandy beaches giving way to sea stacks and wide rock benches riven with channels. These varied habitats host a great diversity of intertidal life, and the relatively shallow slope of the bench means that the usual intertidal zones spread horizontally rather than vertically. Here, the diversity of seaweeds is greater than it is farther south down the coast at Cape Meares, perhaps because sets of sea stacks spare Ecola the harshest of the Pacific waves arriving from the open ocean.

Surfgrass (*Phyllospadix* spp.) is common on low rocky platforms here. A small group of true flowering plants (though not true grasses) inhabiting lower intertidal areas, surfgrasses provide important habitat for invertebrates. Where they are dense, surfgrasses can protect some of the more delicate species by reducing wave forces that might otherwise be intolerable.

The low intertidal rocks at Ecola host hundreds of invertebrate species. Many are hidden from the sun and wind, low amid the overhanging rocks but not so low as to be scoured away by sand. Colonies of various tube worms, sponges, tunicates, and bryozoans colorfully encrust the

Surfgrass (*Phyllospadix* sp.) grows alongside subtidal kelp (*Laminaria setchellii*) at Ecola State Park.

Sand-tolerant species at the low-tide line include encrusting coralline algae, sponges, tunicates, and anemones—a kaleidoscope of color.

hard rock, while nudibranchs and small sea stars (*Leptasterias* spp.) slink among them.

The fine sand here, when inundated, moves like quicksand, capturing visitors' bare feet and gouging out basins around intertidal rocks. These dynamic pools form small habitats that remain submerged, even at the lowest tides, but constant submersion comes at the cost of sand scour. In the sandier areas of Ecola State Park, olive shells, shore crabs, polychaete worms, beach hoppers, and other small crustaceans abound.

At the south end of Ecola State Park lies a series of sea stacks that host seabird colonies. Beyond the brown pelican and western gull, the rocky outcroppings with their relatively flat tops provide nesting habitats for common murres, pigeon guillemots, and cormorants, among others. These are diving seabirds, foraging for fish and other organisms underwater. They can stay submerged for a couple of minutes and dive hundreds of feet, using their wings to propel themselves, essentially flying underwater.

Nesting gulls are here too, and bald eagles perch high in the trees along the shore. In fact, the eagles prey on the nesting birds, flying out to a sea stack and plucking one of thousands from the rocks. Early in the season, before the chicks hatch, eagles tend to eat adult gulls; later, as the young appear, the young ones become the preferred prey of the eagles.

Birds come and go from a colony of common murres (*Uria aalge*) as they care for eggs laid on bare rock.

The iconic Haystack Rock graces Cannon Beach, a popular destination on the Oregon coast.

Just south of Ecola State Park is Cannon Beach, named for a literal (littoral!) cannon that washed up in the late nineteenth century. US Highway 101 went through Cannon Beach until the 1964 tsunami, which washed away the highway and part of the town, forcing the relocation of the highway and providing another example of coastal dynamism. And at Cannon Beach begins the pattern that repeats itself throughout northern Oregon: substantial pocket beaches separated by headlands—and sometimes sea stacks—of volcanic rock.

Haystack Rock is impossible to miss, a 235-foot-tall hunk of volcanic rock nearly 50 percent taller than the state capitol building in Salem. At the foot of this monolith is perhaps the most accessible, and well trampled, rocky habitat in the state. And because of the rock's popularity, Cannon Beach has maintained a Haystack Rock Awareness Program since 1985, complete with uniformed volunteers standing by at summer low tides to protect the habitat and educate passers-by about the rock's

TSUNAMIS

An ocean tsunami is a set of waves caused by the sudden movement of water, generally as a result of an undersea earthquake. These waves move gargantuan volumes of water at speeds of up to 500 miles per hour and can be some of nature's most powerful forces. They are far larger than standard wind-driven waves, and because of their long wavelengths, tsunamis may look more like a fast-rising tide than like a typical breaking wave.

Large tsunamis can be incredibly destructive, wiping out entire sections of coast. The 2004 event in the Indian Ocean, triggered by an exceptionally large earthquake off the coast of Sumatra, devastated coastal communities throughout Indonesia and elsewhere, killing nearly 230,000 people. The 2011 Japanese tsunami followed an earthquake of similar magnitude, killing tens of thousands, damaging approximately a million buildings, and causing nuclear meltdowns at Fukushima.

Tsunamis affecting the US West Coast can be generated by local processes such as underwater landslides or can arise from distant points around the Pacific Rim, triggered by tectonic activity and propagating across the ocean as if it were a bathtub. Quirks of bathymetry then focus the energy of these waves on particular parts of the West Coast so that not every location is subject to the same tsunami risk. The 1964 Alaska earthquake, for example, triggered a tsunami that killed twelve people and destroyed much of the town of Crescent City, California, while leaving many other coastal towns relatively unharmed.

Road signs identify tsunami-evacuation zones along vulnerable parts of the West Coast, and some signs point out routes to the safety of high ground in the event of an earthquake.

tidepools and shorebirds. Haystack Rock is also one of Oregon's seven Marine Gardens, public sites that the state's Department of Fish and Wildlife manages with a focus on education and recreation. (The Marine Gardens span the coastline; north to south, the others are Cape Kiwanda, Otter Rock, Yaquina Head, Yachats State Park, Cape Perpetua, and Harris Beach State Park.)

Just south of Cannon Beach lies Cape Falcon, one of many state marine protected areas. Oswald West State Park occupies the cape and includes the sandy surfing beach at Short Sand Beach, as well as some rocky habitat. This park is somewhat less accessible than its sibling just to the north, with trails leading from US Highway 101 down to the shore where the sandy beach is the main attraction.

Estuaries: Tillamook and Netarts Bays

Shallow and serene, the languid waters of northern Oregon's estuaries let sediment and bits of organic matter settle out of suspension onto the soft bottom. Species that live in the sediment—worms chief among them, along with clams—feed on the edible bits. Birds and fish, in turn, feed on those worms and clams, so that ultimately the organic matter that makes up a good fraction of the soft-bottom habitat itself becomes the energy on which the system feeds.

Tillamook and Netarts Bays, together with Willapa Bay and Grays Harbor in Washington, Coos Bay in southern Oregon, and Humboldt Bay in California, form a chain of soft-sediment habitats that support similar suites of estuarine species along a stretch of more than 500 miles of coastline. These estuaries formed in two different ways in recent geological time: they either are old river valleys—Willapa Bay, Grays Harbor, and Tillamook, Coos, and Humbold Bays—flooded by rising sea levels as ice-age glaciers melted or else, like Netarts Bay, they are captured behind sandbars that have formed in the shallows, creating shelter from the open Pacific.

These and other estuaries experience large swings in temperature and salinity over the course of a day. The species that live in these environments therefore must be tolerant of these kinds of physiological stresses. It's a different kind of stress than that experienced by species on

On the surface, Tillamook Bay looks like a mud desert when the tide is out, but below the surface is an ecosystem teeming with life.

the wave-swept shore, but it is stress nonetheless. The result is a distinct assemblage of species for a distinct habitat.

The worms, clams, and other species that make up these assemblages create three-dimensional habitats in an otherwise flat plain of soft sediment by digging down, generally living most or all of their lives below the surface of the sediment. They then face predictable challenges in eating, excreting, and finding mates while buried underground. These infaunal species solve these challenges in similar ways, often by having long appendages that reach up into the water column to ensnare food (worms, mainly) or by drawing water down to be filtered for food in the main body of the organism (clams). Excretion and mating both tend to happen by shooting waste or gametes, respectively, into the water column while the creature's main body remains hidden. These adaptations are obviously useful for avoiding predators and the other slings and arrows of life above the sediment's surface.

Larger-bodied species are often in evidence too: skates and rays leave circular depressions where they've been foraging in the mud, and unreasonably large moon snails (see Species of Interest in chapter 3,

Washington's Puget Sound and Greater Salish Sea) may sprawl across the mud at low tide.

The calm waters are prime nursery grounds for all kinds of oceangoing fish and crustaceans, including Dungeness crabs (*Metacarcinus magister*, formerly *Cancer magister*). And a host of bird species are regular visitors to mudflats, hunting for marine invertebrates and small fish among the soft sediments and shallow waters.

Estuarine habitats such as Tillamook and Netarts Bays frequently are spots where marine invasive species gain a foothold (see Invasive Species in chapter 2, Living between the Tides). The introduction of invasive species is often a consequence of shipping and other human activities that unintentionally move individuals from place to place, sometimes across great distances. Managing invasive species can present a challenge, especially where they are abundant or noxious—similar to weeds in a garden, invasive species resist efforts to control them.

Managing nonnative species where they invade habitats occupied by their native relatives can be even more challenging. For example, in West Coast estuaries, eelgrass confers a wealth of ecological benefits: it stabilizes substrate, creates organic matter through photosynthesis, and supports a host of associated fish and invertebrates. The native eelgrass (*Zostera marina*) has leaves up to a yard long and can create dense meadows of ecological value in soft-sediment habitats (see Species of Interest in chapter 3). Its invasive relative, the dwarf eelgrass (*Zostera japonica*), also occurs in estuaries between British Columbia and northern California. Dwarf eelgrass was likely introduced to the West Coast alongside oyster spat from Japan in the 1930s. It has finer and much shorter leaves than the native species, offering some but not all of the ecological services provided by the native eelgrass, and it poses a management concern because it can interfere with native species, hinder foraging by shorebirds, and negatively affect shellfish aquaculture.

The Three Capes Scenic Route

Between Rockaway Beach and Neskowin, US Highway 101 heads away from the coast, passing through the town of Tillamook and others to the south. The coastal route here diverges from the highway onto secondary roads that make up the Three Capes Scenic Route. The route skirts three capes and several estuaries, each of which offers something different. Cape Meares and Cape Lookout both are volcanic in origin, featuring steep bluffs below which are intertidal boulders exposed to heavy surf. Cape Meares is particularly notable, being home to one of the largest colonies of nesting seabirds in North America. To the south, Cape Kiwanda is made from sandstone topped by a sand dune, and the story here is all about soft, easily eroded substrates and shifting sands. Interspersed among the three capes are several estuaries that differ in size, shape, depth, and other factors. This relatively short stretch—all told, about forty miles long—offers a diversity of habitats and striking ecological contrasts.

CAPE MEARES

At Cape Meares, the most accessible rocky habitats lie on the north and south sides of the cape, with access via Bayocean Road on the north side and Short Beach off Bayshore Drive on the south side. A rocky shoreline with intermediate to large boulders lies sandwiched between the beach sand and the cliffs of the cape, and even in summer there are likely to be small waterfalls flowing onto the shore below, creating freshwater incursions into the marine realm.

From the north, the rocky foot of the cape offers a varied array of habitat types as beach sand gives way to small boulders, then to pools among larger rocks, and finally to basalt benches—the toes of the cape itself. Shorebirds perch at low tide, hunting, and a great diversity of seaweeds hides invertebrate life in the lower intertidal zone. As elsewhere along the Oregon coast, sand scour can create disturbance among seaweeds and animals, and the rocky-intertidal species that persist here must be able to tolerate the intrusion of sand to some degree.

Acorn barnacles (*Balanus glandula*) are a common feature all along this coast. In places where they are relatively uncrowded, acorn barnacles have a familiar volcano shape, with a broad base and narrow apex. Under very crowded conditions, individuals of the same species tend to develop tall, cylindrical shells that are relatively narrow at the base,

Named for the British explorer John Meares, Cape Meares has steep bluffs that give way to rocky-intertidal habitats.

Under an overhanging rock, a red sponge stands out among barnacles and anemones. Hidden from direct sunlight, the anemones are nearly translucent because they lack pigmented algae in their outer tissue layers.

Many species lay eggs in the lower intertidal zone, and often these egg masses can be easier to spot than the adults that deposited them. Here, snails have left donut-shaped yellow egg masses on algae in the mid intertidal zone.

Barnacle "hummocks" such as these created by the acorn barnacle (*Balanus glandula*) are aggregations in which individuals are packed so densely that they change their growth form, shifting from the typical volcano shape to tall, thin columns. Disturbance in these tightly packed aggregations can remove many individuals at once, creating bare patches and opening space for others.

looking more like an architectural column than a volcano. These densely packed tall barnacles often form hummocks that appear to make it easier for individuals to capture food and withstand temperature and desiccation stresses, while leaving them susceptible to disturbances that remove whole patches of barnacles at once, creating gaps that other species quickly occupy. Hummocks can create habitat for small-bodied limpets, snails, chitons, and other species that find shelter in the interior niches among individual barnacles.

Seabirds are common in the vicinity of Cape Meares: like other prominent headlands, the cape offers solid ground in a location valuable for its proximity to abundant nearshore food sources. Just as we might expect an increase in diversity of invertebrates among the rocks of headlands, we might also expect a diversity of seabird predators on those invertebrates. Schools of small fish, too, gather near rocky outcroppings, attracting further attention from birds. Consequently, most headlands along the West

Coast feature oystercatchers, peeping and puttering among the boulders as they seek a meal. Sandpipers zip in formation along wet sand flats, occasionally rising into the air in coordinated flocks. Cormorants, perched and almost disdainful, dry their wings and supervise. Gulls, among the most conspicuous of seabirds, use both rocky and sandy shores, and are notoriously difficult to tell apart. Sea ducks, too, are common around Cape Meares (see Species of Interest later in this chapter).

CAPE LOOKOUT

Situated between Cape Meares and Cape Kiwanda, Cape Lookout is perhaps the most prominent geological feature along this stretch of coastline. Volcanic in origin, the cape is a product of the Columbia River basalt flow of about 15.5 million years ago. Erosion of the cape over eons has contributed to the formation of the long sandy spit to the north that forms the seaward edge of Netarts Bay. Long, narrow, and tall, the cape offers good views from the Cape Lookout Trail that runs its length. This is a good vantage point for seeing gray whales during their annual migration.

A geologic remnant of ancient lava flows, Cape Lookout (in the distance) extends about two miles due west into the Pacific Ocean.

The northern kelp crab (*Pugettia producta*) can be purplish, dark brown, or olive green. As might be expected from its common name, it typically hangs out in kelp beds but can be found in the intertidal. Its pinch can be fierce.

Steep cliffs make access to the rocky intertidal difficult and dangerous in most places. The most accessible rocky habitat is located near the base of the cape on its north side. Here, steeply sloping bedrock gives way to large boulders, providing habitat for invertebrates and seaweeds that can tolerate extreme wave exposure and shifting sands. The surrounding beach sands are home to a completely different suite of species, prominent among which are sand crabs, beach hoppers, and small isopods.

Two red seaweeds growing nearly side by side at Cape Lookout illustrate some of the fascinating (and sometimes frustrating) diversity among seaweeds. The deep-red blades of *Schizymenia pacifica* are roughly oval in shape and are often cleft—hence, the origin of the genus name. One of their chief identifying characteristics is their slippery feel. The blades found growing on low intertidal rocks are annual—that is, just like annual plants, they last for only one season. In between times, *Schizymenia* persists as a low-growing, crustose form that is so different it was at first thought to be a distinct species, *Haematocelis*. Sharing a similar habitat, the red seaweed *Ptilota filicina* is quite different: it's finely branched, lives for more than one year, and doesn't have an alternate cryptic stage.

A red seaweed (*Ptilota filicina*) grows on a rocky face below a band of aggregating anemones. The seaweed has fine, fern-like branching, as reflected in the species name *filicina*.

A sandy intertidal zone is a canvas, wiped clean twice daily by tides and polished by the wind. Ephemeral tracks in the sand, then, reflect the comings and goings of animal species over the course of hours. A close look rewards the coastal visitor by revealing activity even when the animals themselves remain hidden. Most often, small tracks on drying sand are the work of small-bodied crustaceans such as amphipods (hoppers), isopods, sand crabs (also called mole crabs), juvenile true crabs of many kinds, and other shell-bearing relatives. Traces from molluscs such as the purple olive shell (*Callianax biplicata*, formerly *Olivella biplicata*) and worms like the polychaete catworm (family Nephtyidae) are also common, as are those of shorebirds or larger-bodied animals such as raccoons, hunting to make a meal of these invertebrates. And although animal tracks are nearly always short-lived, in some exceptional circumstances such as volcanic eruptions or slumping events triggered by earthquakes, these tracks get preserved in the fossil record: the discipline of paleoecology aims to untangle ancient interactions among species, in part by using the fossilized tracks like those we see today in the sand.

Different species leave tracks of varying shapes and sizes in wet sand. Here, a purple olive snail (*Callianax biplicata*, formerly *Olivella biplicata*) cuts a wandering swath.

CAPE KIWANDA

Cape Kiwanda is visibly different from other rocky habitats in northern Oregon. Made entirely of sandstone, the cape likely would have disappeared long ago, whittled away by wave action, if not for the protection of Chief Kiawanda Rock (also known as Haystack Rock) just offshore. This large feature is made of more durable basalt and in the distant past was likely connected with the sandstone formation that makes up Cape Kiwanda. Over geologic time, the basalt feature has endured, while the sandstone formation that once connected the two has slowly disappeared into the sea.

Cape Kiwanda is one of seven intertidal areas on the Oregon coast designated as a Marine Garden, and the soft substrate here supports a host of intertidal species. On the south side of the cape, deep fissures create miniature canyons whose walls are covered by invertebrates. Seaweeds and invertebrates carpet the steep sides of these rocks, whose flat tops are

The sandstone bluff of Cape Kiwanda points toward Chief Kiawanda Rock offshore. The two features were once attached.

often bare. Carved sandstone bowls capture seawater and create pools of different sizes and tidal heights. Sculpins and crabs do well in these pools, alternately foraging and hiding from predators.

Species that tolerate sand scour and inundation are prominent here. Among these is the kelp *Laminaria sinclairii*. This kelp is unusual: instead of the single stipe and holdfast common to most of its relatives, *L. sinclairii* produces a dense system of horizontal stem-like rhizomes that give rise to multiple stipes and blades. The stipes are perennial, lasting year upon year, while the blades are annual, disappearing and regrowing each year, a seasonal pattern that is much like that of deciduous shrubs. The rhizomes of *L. sinclairii* are attached to rocks that are often buried in sand. This unusual lifestyle may be an adaptation to disturbance in sand-inundated areas.

The green seaweed *Codium setchellii* found in the low intertidal here is an odd thing. Nearly black in color and with a spongy, brain-like appearance and texture, the seaweed consists of a dense network of filaments.

Its curious morphology makes it very effective at absorbing sunlight, and its low-growing form is tolerant of wave action.

The California mussels (*Mytilus californianus*) here grow to be the size of a shoe and are densely packed together. This suggests that they live long lives and have plenty to eat. Space for fresh recruits can be difficult to come by, but as the soft sandstone erodes due to disturbance, new space opens up for settlement.

Aside from the biology and geology on display here, the Pacific City dory fleet is active, using the sandy beach and protected cove south of Cape Kiwanda to launch and land its affiliated boats. Dory operators trailer their flat-bottomed boats onto the beach, back them into the waves, and head out to sea over the waves, doing the reverse on their return. For more than a hundred years, the dory fishing fleet has operated from this spot to fish for the salmon, tuna, rockfish, and crab that occupy the waters offshore, offering evidence of regional productivity that extends well beyond the intertidal zone.

Juvenile California mussels (*Mytilus californianus*) that claim a bare patch of rock (center) are black, unlike older mussels that, with other organisms, surround them.

Fogarty Creek

Different from the massive headlands to the north, Fogarty Creek features smooth, rounded rocks and benches that create interesting intertidal habitat. The intertidal bench is most expansive on the south side of the beach, across US Highway 101 from the parking lot at Fogarty Creek State Recreation Area.

The rocky intertidal habitat at Fogarty Creek differs from those not far to the south at Yaquina Head, Yachats, and Strawberry Hill. For starters, the intertidal here consists mostly of sedimentary rocks (sandstone, siltstone, and mudstone), in contrast to the volcanic substrates found farther south. These sedimentary substrates tend to offer poorer footholds for invertebrates and seaweeds because they are more easily eroded by wave action; for animals, it can be a tough place to hang on for long.

Here, too, oceanographic factors play a role: the ocean supports less primary production than in areas to the south, meaning that phytoplankton and the food it supplies are less abundant. Invertebrate larvae don't tend to recruit here in the large numbers they do elsewhere, perhaps as a result of the diminished food supply. And local long-shore transport tends to isolate Fogarty Creek from beaches to the north and south; this is reflected in the fine-grained beach sand, which differs from the coarser-grained sands on other beaches in the region.

What's immediately apparent here is the amount of bare space in the mid intertidal, especially in winter. While mid intertidal rocks at other sites can be jammed with long-lived invertebrates and seaweeds vying for rare space, here the most abundant commodity is open space itself. To ecologists, bare space can be just as interesting as densely packed spaces: Why are densities so low? What processes are at play? At this site, the combination of low ocean productivity and soft, erodible substrates are part of the story, along with the seasonal nature of seaweed cover, which can be dense in summer and sparse in winter.

These relatively soft substrates are favored by some intertidal species. Boring clams, bivalve molluscs in the family Pholadidae, use their shells to grind holes in soft rocks. They then occupy the burrow for their entire

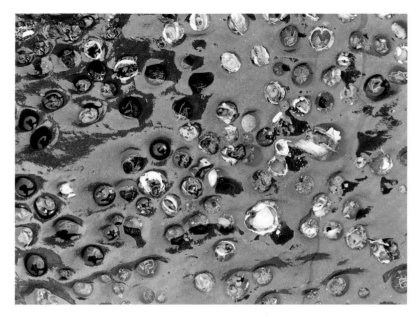

Boring clams (family *Pholadidae*), also known as rough piddocks, inhabit self-made burrows in soft rock. Here, many are dead, evident from broken and exposed white shells (upper- and middle-right); these may have been crushed by forces associated with winter storms. But small specimens of living clams are visible too (bottom and left). A close look reveals fecal castings in some burrows, a sure sign of a living clam within.

life, with only a siphon extended for purposes of feeding. Once the clam dies, other species sometimes take up residence in the vacated burrow.

In many places the soft stone bench is dimpled with potholes. These form when small hard concretions erode out of the larger parent rock but remain trapped in shallow depressions. Over time, water motion causes the cobble to wear away the walls of its rocky entrapment, further entraining the cobble and enlarging the pothole. Eventually, some potholes lose their cobbles, and the depression becomes a home for organisms such as the giant green anemone.

In the lower intertidal zone, space is more densely occupied. Kelps, especially the sea cabbage (*Hedophyllum sessile*), are abundant, as are red seaweeds of several different species. At the most seaward edge of the

The lined chiton (*Tonicella lineata*) is common in high-energy intertidal environments from Alaska to northern California.

The kelp known as sea cabbage (*Hedophyllum sessile*) is unusual because it has no stipe. A young individual's finger-like appendages called *haptera* (here, yellowish) cement it to the substrate.

rocky bench, you might find the kelp *Lessoniopsis littoralis*. This kelp is notable for its inflexible massive woody stipe, which allows the seaweed to persist year upon year in exposed locations subject to heavy surf. At other sites, *Lessoniopsis* sometimes shares these wave-swept habitats with the sea palm (*Postelsia palmaeformis*). The two species take opposite approaches to coping with extreme wave action: *Lessoniopsis*, which lives many years, invests in rigid thick big stipes that withstand wave forces, while *Postelsia* lives only a single season, building hollow, flexible stipes that bend with the flow, shedding the force of breaking waves.

Yaquina Head

Yaquina Head looks like a giant serrated hunting knife jutting out from the coastline, slicing through expanses of sandy beach on either side. Located just north of Newport, the largest town on the Oregon coast, this is one of the more accessible spots around, and it's a great place to see birds and marine mammals as well as tidepool denizens. This site is one of Oregon's Marine Gardens, special places that are dedicated to conservation and public education. A naturalist is often on hand at the beach, guided tours may be available, and an interpretive center is located nearby.

Below the lighthouse parking lot, the site features a cobble beach on the south side of the headland, leading to a rocky bench in the lower reaches of the intertidal zone. Different from those to the north at Fogarty Creek, the bench here is volcanic in origin. In early spring, the mid intertidal areas look fuzzy and reddish, covered by low-growing red algal turfs. Turfs are tough, and although they are natural parts of intertidal communities, they also can be a sign of physical disturbance. A long list of other seaweed species has been recorded from this site, including several kelp species and seasonally occurring red and green algae.

Invertebrates here include those commonly found along the coast: mussels, barnacles, urchins, and sea stars, along with anemones, snails, chitons, hermit crabs, and a host of more cryptic species. Great blue herons forage in the intertidal here (see Birds of Protected Waters later in this chapter). Long channels carved into the bench create varied habitat that supports this diversity.

Just offshore lie South Rocks, Seal Rock, and Lion's Head. These low rocky outcrops are favored haul-outs for pinnipeds. Harbor seals are resident here, and Steller sea lions, California sea lions, and northern elephant seals are occasional visitors. Offshore, gray whales, orcas, minke

Motile invertebrates, like this purple urchin (*Strongylocentrotus purpuratus*), take cover beneath seaweed or in cracks and crevices among the rocks, presumably as a means of avoiding predation.

Prominent offshore rocks support a host of seabird species. Guano produced by seabirds contributes recycled nitrogen to nearshore systems, boosting productivity.

The Yaquina Head lighthouse towers over the shore at Yaquina Head Outstanding Natural Area.

whales, Dall's porpoises, and harbor porpoises all have been spotted (see Marine Mammals in chapter 6, The Southern Oregon Coast).

The offshore rocks provide habitat for birds, too, some of which use the area for nesting, while others are just passing through. In early spring, common murres are distinctly audible—their calls are unmistakable—and with some searching visitors will find them on the water or perhaps at a nest site. In summer look for brown pelicans, identifiable by their large size and prominent long bill. Cormorants are common here, too, and all three West Coast species—Brandt's, double-crested, and pelagic—have been reported. At least ten species of gull have been sited at Yaquina Head, and many species are likely to be present at a given time. For all these species, see Birds of the Exposed Coast later in this chapter.

A more sheltered, engineered habitat lies just east of the cobble beach, via the Quarry Cove Trail or from a separate parking lot. Constructed at the site of a former rock quarry that provided building materials for

US Highway 101 during much of the twentieth century, the Quarry Cove habitat was constructed by the US Bureau of Land Management to replicate an intertidal habitat, albeit with amenities including a wheelchair-accessible footpath.

SPECIES OF INTEREST

Worms

Different types of worms often can be identified by the shapes of their burrow holes and castings around those holes. It can be great fun to do a bit of detective work in the mudflats in spite of the mud and muck. For example, the Pacific lugworm (*Abarenicola pacifica*) creates a spiral-shaped pile of its castings directly on top of its J-shaped burrow. The red-banded bamboo worm (*Axiothella rubrocincta*) creates a tube of sediment that can stick up off of the substrate at low tide; in some cases, the worm's tube also hosts a very tiny pea crab (*Pinnixa longipes*). A little digging may unearth pile worms (*Nereis vexillosa*), which can grow to be a foot long and have fierce-looking black jaws. Superficially similar, with many shimmering lobe-like appendages, is the giant clam bed worm (*Alitta brandti*)–but this one can be up to five feet long and may accordingly fuel nightmares. Both species swim into the water column in large aggregations to spawn in summer. Others are less imposing, or less colorful, but still contribute to the literally hundreds of species of worms that make a living in the soft-sediment habitats of the West Coast.

Sand Crab

On many sandy beaches, sand crabs (*Emerita analoga*), also known as mole crabs, come in droves when the water recedes, quickly burying themselves back-end first to leave their stalked eyes and feathery antennae poking out of the sand in the waves' swash zone. They make conspicuous V shapes in the sand as a wave recedes, so you can see exactly where they are. Scoop them up and have a close-up look: the bigger ones can be more than an inch long, and many of the females carry bright orange eggs on their underside. These widespread, common residents

Sand crabs (*Emerita analoga*), also called mole crabs, hurry to bury themselves as wave swash recedes.

of sandy habitats are an important food source for larger fishes and for shorebirds including willets, godwits, curlews, and plovers.

Brittle Stars

A seashore visitor, on finding beneath an overturned rock a tangle of spaghetti-like arms covered in stiff bristles, might well wonder how such frenetic, delicate-looking things can live for long in such a habitat. And yet for millions of years, brittle stars have endured.

These relatives of sea stars resemble their stouter cousins, insofar as they generally have five arms radiating out from a central disc, on which are located their mouths and other important bits. But where sea stars are hearty enough to take a punch from oncoming waves, brittle stars would fall to pieces. And in part, this is a strategy: they lose arms easily, a mechanism for escaping from predators, and quickly regrow those arms later. Each arm is loaded with hydraulic tube feet (as are sea stars' arms, although brittle stars' tube feet lack suckers and aren't as conspicuous).

At least five species of brittle stars hide in the more protected waters of the Pacific Northwest, but the dwarf brittle star (*Amphipholis squamata*)

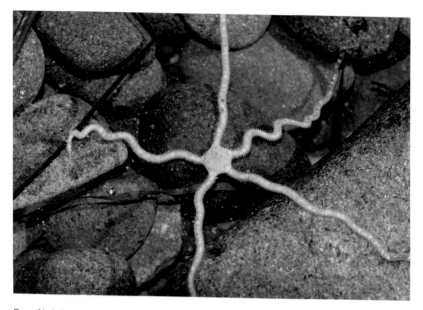

Dwarf brittle stars (*Amphipholis* spp.) are common in tidepools, yet as their name suggests, they need to shelter under rocks or other hard surfaces to protect themselves from waves and other disturbance. Photo by Jerry Kirkhart CC-BY-2.0.

deserves special mention. The disc of this species is less than a quarter inch across, yet it broods its young, carrying up to twenty-five even tinier stars around in armpit pockets. And as if this wasn't interesting enough, the species is also bioluminescent, producing a ghostly greenish light along the lengths of its fragile arms.

Birds of the Exposed Coast

Birds, in general, are the objects of fascination and even obsession for people in all walks of life; seabirds are a small subset of this wider winged world, but they can be among the flashier and more dynamic of life-forms along the shore. And from the point of view of intertidal invertebrates, different bird species are often fearsome predators; to a limpet, a black oystercatcher is death from above. Hence, shorebirds often occupy the upper reaches of coastal food webs, even if they don't appear particularly threatening to us.

SOOTY SHEARWATER

Spring to fall, dark, attractive sooty shearwaters (*Ardenna grisea*, formerly *Puffinus griseus*) hunt small squids, anchovies, and other species along the outer coasts of the Pacific Northwest before returning to their breeding grounds in isolated coastal areas of the southern hemisphere. Shearwaters are relatives of the albatross and, like them, have prominent tube-shaped nostrils thought to help them excrete salt.

BROWN PELICAN

The unmistakable form of the brown pelican (*Pelecanus occidentalis*) graces the West Coast and many other western-hemisphere coastlines as it dives for fish and glides among the waves on a wingspan that can top seven feet. Pelicans dive steeply into the water to scoop up fish and other prey in their large throat pouches. This species experienced especially steep losses as a result of the industrial pesticide DDT and was federally protected under the Endangered Species Act until 2009. Its recovery, a direct result of the 1972 ban on DDT, is a clear-cut success story for environmental management and for marine ecology.

CORMORANTS

Three species of cormorants ply the region's waters: Brandt's (*Urile penicillatus*), pelagic (*U. pelagicus*), and double-crested (*Nannopterum auritum*), all formerly in the genus *Phalacrocorax*. Visitors commonly see these diving birds squatting on rocks or pilings, watchful with their distinctive dark bodies and long necks. Or if they have their wings out, they are drying damp feathers—the lack of water-repellent feathers would seem an unfortunate oversight for a diving bird. These birds are sleek underwater hunters, appearing quite at home as they zip among fishes, frosted with bubbles.

BALD EAGLE

Our national symbol, the bald eagle (*Haliaeetus leucocephalus*) is another conservation success story, having rebounded like the brown pelican after the ban on DDT and also having recovered under the Endangered Species

Act. Even as bald eagles have become more common in the Pacific Northwest, they never fail to inspire: they are instantly recognizable, powerfully built, and massive. With wingspans of more than seven feet and nests that could sleep several adult humans, these are the world's largest raptors as measured from tip to tail. They nest in mature trees quite near the water's edge, eating salmon or other substantial fish, juvenile otters or other mammals, or indeed, essentially anything they want.

PLOVERS

Plovers (genus *Charadrius*) are small shorebirds that migrate to and from the Arctic, but one of the four or so species that occur in the Pacific Northwest, the killdeer (*C. vociferus*), is a year-round resident. Their coloration makes plovers difficult to track as they hunt for insects and other small prey along the shore, but famously, several species have behavior designed to be noticed: by faking injury and making noise, adult birds can distract intruders away from their ground-level nests.

BLACK OYSTERCATCHER

The sturdy bright-red beak of the black oystercatcher (*Haematopus bachmani*) pops out against the bird's dark plumage and the brown palette of its rocky intertidal habitat, as do its school-bus-yellow irises. This bird eats almost entirely invertebrates from among shoreline rocks, its beak strong enough to break or pry apart the shells of mussels, limpets, and the like.

GULLS

Humanity's environmental alterations have tended to favor species that are ecological generalists—that is, those that might live comfortably in a variety of conditions, eating a variety of foods, and so on. Gulls fit this description, seemingly ubiquitous at coastal sites and as likely to be found eating out of a trash can as diving into a school of nearshore fish. About a dozen species of gulls live or migrate through the coastal Pacific Northwest. The glaucous-winged gull (*Larus glaucescens*) and the western gull (*L. occidentalis*), each with a wingspan approaching five feet, are

Black oystercatchers (*Haematopus bachmani*) are recognizable by their long red bill. They tend to feed on mussels, limpets, urchins, whelks, and other invertebrates, but—curiously—not oysters.

year-round residents and likely to be the most common. The western gull is the most abundant gull species in Oregon, nesting on offshore islands and coastal rocks. Western gulls forage both at sea, where they take fish and pelagic invertebrates, and in the intertidal, where they feed on a range of benthic invertebrates.

COMMON MURRE

The common murre (*Uria aalge*) forms large colonies along the Pacific coast—for example, Oregon's Yaquina Head hosts tens of thousands of individuals. Also members of the auk family, common murres spend most of their life at sea, coming to shore to nest on ledges or cliff tops where they produce a single egg laid in a shallow depression, without nest material. Their streamlined shape tells us something about their habits: they can dive to depths of several hundred feet and they pursue prey of small fishes. Murres use their wings for propulsion to swim underwater, flying through the depths in search of fish.

PIGEON GUILLEMOT

The pigeon guillemot (*Cepphus columba*) nests among rocky cliffs near shorelines, where it feeds on small fishes in the shallow intertidal. As the name implies, these birds look something like a large dark pigeon but are not pigeons at all—they're really a species of auk. They are recognizable by the wedge of white on their wings and—most noticeably—their bright red feet and red mouth framed by a prominent black bill. Their breeding plumage is a uniform very dark brown broken by the white wing patches. Pigeon guillemots form long-term bonds with their mates and are able to swim underwater using their short wings for propulsion.

TUFTED PUFFIN

The world's largest puffin—which isn't saying much, as they grow to just over a foot long—is the tufted puffin (*Fratercula cirrhata*). But what they lack in size, they make up in character, sporting prominent red beaks and charismatic yellow tufts on each side of their head that grow annually for the summer breeding season and molt off afterward. Puffins are in the auk family, along with murres, guillemots, and a few others, and they share with these a remarkable underwater agility, which they use to hunt fish, squid, krill, and other marine animals. The birds move offshore to feed in winter, nesting on isolated marine islands in the Pacific Northwest during summer.

Birds of Protected Waters

GREAT BLUE HERON

Coming upon a great blue heron (*Ardea herodias*) is not unusual in the Pacific Northwest, but every time it happens, it seems distinctly like watching a dinosaur in action. This bird is huge, standing more than four feet tall with a wingspan approaching six feet, and its silent, still manner is both arresting and slightly unnerving. Herons are stealthy wading birds. Visual predators, they stand motionless, heads cantilevered out away from their bodies, waiting for prey to happen by. Or else they walk agonizingly slowly in search of a meal, which they quickly dispatch and swallow whole. Widely distributed and often found in freshwater habitats far from the coast, the coastal herons feed on small fish such as sticklebacks, gunnels, and sculpins.

GEESE

Geese (family Anatidae) are familiar large birds in many regions, and the Canada goose (*Branta canadensis*) in particular has made a home alongside human settlements to such an extent that it is often considered a pest. Brants (*B. bernicla*) and snow geese (*Anser caerulescens*, formerly *Chen caerulescens*) are also common in the Pacific Northwest. All of these geese are vegetarians, eating seagrass, sea lettuce, and other vegetable matter in shallow, protected habitats.

DUCKS

Ducks belong to the same family (Anatidae) as geese and swans. These waterbirds are adapted for swimming, feeding, and even diving in shallow waters. Among the ducks, familial divisions reflect ecological differences. Washington and Oregon have representatives from the dabbling ducks (the familiar mallard, teal, gadwall, and others), the diving ducks (scaups), and sea ducks (goldeneye, bufflehead, harlequin, scoter, and merganser), among others. The harlequin duck (*Histrionicus histrionicus*) is notable for its colorful plumage; its name comes from the Latin for "theatrical." Harlequins are at home in rough water, both along the exposed coasts that constitute their wintering habitat and in fast-flowing mountain streams where they breed. In coastal areas they feed on molluscs and crustaceans.

AMERICAN COOT

A black wetland bird shaped like a small hen, the American coot (*Fulica americana*) has a white bill and endearingly odd feet with lobe-shaped webbing. Also known as mud hens, these birds are common alongside ducks in protected waters of the Pacific Northwest, where they are strong divers and swimmers. They eat predominately vegetable matter in shallow habitats and may also include small invertebrates in their diets.

SANDPIPERS

Many species of sandpiper (family Scolopacidae) live or migrate along the Pacific Northwest coast, and as a rule, these are quick sand-colored birds that make a living by poking their long bills into sand or mud in search of an invertebrate meal. Small crustaceans and worms, being the most common animals living in these habitats, are generally sandpipers' targets, but different bird species have bills of different lengths, allowing them to avoid competing for precisely the same food. Those larger-bodied species with longer bills, such as the long-billed curlew (*Numenius americanus*), which winters along the West Coast, can extract larger prey out of deeper burrows.

COMMON TERN

The beautiful, streamlined common tern (*Sterna hirundo*) breeds at locations all around the northern hemisphere; those along our coast belong to a North American subspecies and are migrants. Terns dive for small fish just offshore, their orange legs and bills contrasting neatly with their black-white-gray bodies.

COMMON CROW

The common crow (*Corvus brachyrhynchos*) is not a seabird, but it is common enough along Pacific shores that it is likely to play important ecological roles at intertidal sites. These birds, iridescent black with a look of trouble in their eyes, are frighteningly smart, able to use tools to solve problems and to recognize and remember the behavior of individual humans. They are omnivores, well accustomed to living alongside humans, but also quite able to feed on molluscs, crustaceans, and worms at the shore. The common raven (*Corvus corax*), the crow's larger and less-common cousin, is also found in the region.

Beachcast kelp in northern Oregon

Cannon Beach on a gray day

North of Gold Beach, Oregon

THE
SOUTHERN
OREGON
COAST

Rising a fraction of an inch each year relative to sea level, the southern half of Oregon's coast is being pushed up from below as the last bit of the Juan de Fuca plate burrows underneath North America (see Tectonics and Subduction in chapter 1, The Tumultuous Earth). Some of the most productive waters in the state are found in this region, especially around Cape Perpetua, supporting a huge array of life as favorable upwelling conditions (see Coastal Upwelling in chapter 1) bring abundant nutrients to shore. Nutrients fuel the growth of phytoplankton and seaweeds, and these in turn become food for animals. For many species, more food translates into having more offspring, so that more productivity at the base of the food web means more biomass throughout the food web (see Nutrients, Oxygen, and Carbon Dioxide in chapter 2, Living between the Tides). For example, barnacles can be five times more fecund in southern Oregon than at other sites along the Oregon coast, which translates into lots of barnacles and also a lot of larvae that become food for other species. This is a land of abundance, and the tidepools reflect that.

The young rocks and rolling topography of the Oregon Coast Range accompany travelers throughout much of a drive along the southern Oregon coast, with basalt headlands and sandy beaches continuing the large-scale patterns seen in chapter 5, The Northern Oregon Coast. This general

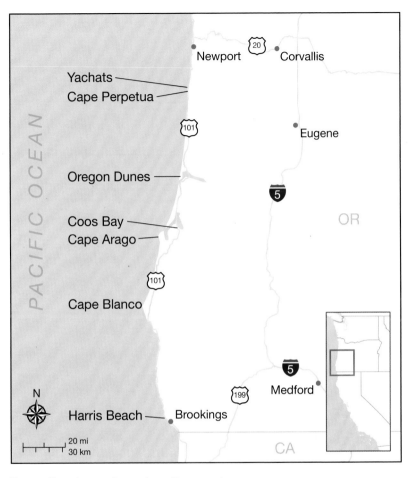

Featured locations on Oregon's southern coast

pattern is interrupted by the Oregon dunes, an expansive temperate coastal sand dune stretching for more than fifty miles along the coast from Florence to Coos Bay. This massive complex of sand ridges and valleys is one of the largest of its kind in the world, supporting different kinds of plants and animals than is typical of the rest of the Oregon coast and attracting humans with off-road vehicles and a thirst for adrenaline.

The Coast Range gives way to the older Siskiyou Mountains only at the very southern corner of the state. From Bandon south into California, the coast is backed by the Siskiyous, whose bedrock, at around 150 million years old, give or take, is some of the oldest in Oregon. And the makeup of the Siskiyous is different too, consisting mostly of metamorphic rock sloping steeply into the sea. Rocky islands and towering sea stacks loom offshore, and tidepool life is vibrant and dynamic wherever there is suitable rocky habitat.

PLACES TO EXPLORE
Yachats

The charming town of Yachats straddles an eponymous small river and estuary. The town sits on top of a marine terrace whose basalt bench is exposed at the coastline, running the length of the town and beyond. The rocks here, known as Yachats basalt, are the northern edge of a coastline produced by undersea and terrestrial lava flows more than 30 million years ago. Yachats basalt extends north to Yaquina Head and south to Cape Perpetua and Strawberry Hill, taking on different appearances in each location, partly owing to the source of the lava and how quickly the lava cooled after its release. Over time, weather and waves have continually reshaped these rock formations. Sandy areas interspersed among them create mosaics of intertidal habitats that are rich with species.

On the north side of the Yachats River, the 804 Trail provides easy and scenic access to a varied stretch of beach. Right near the trail's parking lot is Smelt Sands Beach itself, a small pocket beach that, as its name implies, is a favored spawning site for surf smelt. These small schooling fish, which occur from Alaska to California, prefer sites with coarse sand and fine gravel in upper intertidal areas for spawning. The red seaweed *Ahnfeltiopsis* occupies the same sort of sand and gravel substrates used by surf smelt. With its stiff, tough branches, this seaweed tolerates sand scour, even burial, and tends to live only in habitats that are intermittently inundated by sand.

From the parking lot, the 804 Trail (named for a road that in the last century linked Yachats and Waldport) heads north from the Surf Smelt Sand Recreation Site on the northern end of Yachats, meandering along a low bluff. Ebb tide reveals low-lying rounded basalt rocks that eons

The coarse sand and small pebbles of Smelt Sands Beach are the favored spawning habitat of the surf smelt (*Hypomesus pretiosus*). The red seaweed here (foreground) is *Ahnfeltiopsis*, a species unusually tolerant of sand scour and burial; the smooth black rocks (background) are a good example of Yachats basalt.

of wave and sand scour have polished smooth. Many of the taller rock formations have flat tops and steep sides. Relatively little life clings to the tops of these formations because few species can tolerate the combination of surf, scour, sun exposure, and human foot traffic. Those that can tolerate these conditions tend to be seasonal or ephemeral occupants, growing quickly and disappearing just as quickly.

In contrast, the vertical faces of these rocks harbor high densities of long-lived animals that are suspension-feeders, prominent among which are California mussels (see Species of Interest in this chapter) and gooseneck barnacles (see Species of Interest on the Rocky Northern Coast in chapter 4, Washington's Outer Coast). Close inspection of the gooseneck barnacles will reveal limpets living on the barnacles' calcareous plates. One such limpet species (*Lottia digitalis*) has a barnacle-associated form

A fingered limpet (*Lottia digitalis*) is cryptic here (middle-left) among the calcareous plates of a gooseneck barnacle. Smaller black limpets (*Lottia asmi*) are more easily seen here—two are in the middle to the right of the fingered limpet.

that mimics the coloration of the barnacles and is quite cryptic, while its relative (*Lottia asmi*) is smaller but, because it is dark and doesn't match the barnacles, is more obvious.

Space for attachment is clearly limiting on these vertical rock faces; as in a rain forest, there is something growing on nearly everything. Barnacles cover the shells of densely packed mussels, and predatory snails move in to eat the barnacles. Limpets take up residence on the backs of the snails and mussels. Seaweeds are rare in these assemblages, likely because they can't compete for space or are quickly consumed by grazing invertebrates. The entire community is fueled by favorable upwelling conditions that are common along this stretch of coastline.

Continuing northward along the 804 Trail offers more opportunities to observe these wave-swept, rocky intertidal communities, eventually ending at a sandy beach. Alternatively, visitors can head south along the trail from the parking lot toward the heart of Yachats to the river mouth and its sandy estuary, accessible at low tide.

The view from the Cape Perpetua Overlook offers a glimpse of the coastal geology, with the highway cut into the steep slope of the coastal mountains where they meet the sea. Waves from offshore begin to break as the water becomes shallower, hinting at the shape of the bottom just under the surface.

Cape Perpetua

Dramatic rocky headlands are common along the Oregon coast, and the Cape Perpetua area is one of these, offering numerous opportunities for tidepooling, beach walking, and hiking. Part of the Siuslaw National Forest, it sits right in the middle of Oregon just south of Yachats and boasts nearly 3,000 acres of old-growth forest. Nearly thirty miles of trails feature a classic coastal forest: a mix of Douglas fir, western hemlock, and Sitka spruce (see Species of Interest on the Rocky Northern Coast in chapter 4, Washington's Outer Coast).

STRAWBERRY HILL

Only a short distance south from Cape Perpetua and Yachats, Strawberry Hill offers several sharp contrasts to its more northerly neighbors. Part of the Neptune State Scenic Viewpoint, Strawberry Hill is accessible via a turnout along US Highway 101 near milepost 169. The beach here is backed by an eroding high bluff composed of distinct sedimentary layers, evidence of the geological past. The bluff gives way to a field of rounded small cobbles and coarse sand. The sand contains a high proportion of shell fragments, suggesting the large numbers of shelled invertebrates that have lived and died here, perhaps during winter storms, which can impose an enormous amount of destructive energy, with waves mobilizing sand and turning cobbles into projectiles that pummel, crush, and grind. The sand and cobble beach yields to a broad, low rocky bench that is deeply cut by sand-filled channels.

Stairs from the parking lot lead both north and south, and either choice offers a nice expanse of rocky habitat at low tide. A cool-morning low tide might reveal harbor seals lounging on the outer fringes of the rocky platform and gulls foraging for invertebrates that have been exposed by the receding water. Indeed, evidence of predation may be apparent, with piles of shell debris scattered about.

Sand shapes this intertidal community. Seasonal inundation by sand alternately buries and uncovers living organisms, and those that persist tend to be tough enough to withstand regular sand scour and burial.

Relatively flat rocky benches at Strawberry Hill support communities strongly influenced by sand.

Piles of shell debris offer clues about the predators nearby. Crushed mollusc shells may result from crabs' powerful claws or from birds dropping intact mussels and snails from a height, using gravity and the ground to break into the shell. Drill holes more likely reflect a molluscan predator, such as a whelk or even an octopus.

Several species of red seaweed are among those that do well here. One of these is a species (*Neorhodomela larix*) that forms dense low turfs in intertidal areas. *Neorhodomela* isn't restricted to sandy habitats—it will grow perfectly well in the absence of sand—but it has the advantage of being able to tolerate long periods of burial and the accompanying scour and anoxia that sand burial produces, while its competitors and predators are less tolerant of these conditions.

Other seaweeds take the opposite strategy for dealing with sand. For example, instead of becoming tough and resistant to sand scour, the brown seaweed *Phaeostrophion* produces relatively delicate short-lived blades, avoiding the investment required to build tougher tissues. This is, in fact, a general ecological strategy that calls to mind Kleenex: structures that are cheap to produce, useful when you need them, and disposable once they are no longer useful. In the case of *Phaeostrophion*, the blades tend to emerge in the colder months and disappear during warmer months. Key to the persistence of this species is its ability to produce a

A red seaweed (*Neorhodomela larix*), with its tough whorled branches, is a good example of a sand-tolerant species.

At the offshore edge of a rocky platform, common invertebrates fill every available space, and the positions of different species reflect the ecological niche of each. For example, those nearer the bottom (sea anemones) must tolerate a degree of sand scour. Those in the middle must somehow avoid being eaten by the predatory and mobile sea stars. Those nearer the top (barnacles and mussels) must be able to survive longer warm and dry periods out of water.

low-growing crustose phase that persists year-round and gives rise to new generations of blades.

At the offshore edge of the flat bench are rocks of slightly higher relief. On this outer edge there tends to be less sand, and the dominant community is the familiar one of mussels, barnacles, sea stars, invertebrate grazers, and big anemones, all in abundance. Their density reflects favorable ocean conditions that provide plenty of planktonic food and a reliable source of larvae.

BOB CREEK

Just to the south of Strawberry Hill lies Bob Creek, at US Highway 101 milepost 170. The southernmost site in the Neptune State Scenic Viewpoint, it is separated from Strawberry Hill by a small rocky promontory. Many features here are similar to those at Strawberry Hill, including a cobble field in the high intertidal adjacent to a sandy beach punctuated

The intertidal at Bob Creek is a mixture of cobble, sand, and rocky bench; the rocky bench supports familiar invertebrate and algal species.

by low rocky benches at the north and south ends. And with similar habitat comes similar species—Bob Creek offers a reflection of the intertidal communities found at Strawberry Hill.

As at Strawberry Hill, many of the organisms visitors find at Bob Creek tolerate sand. The mossy chiton (*Mopalia muscosa*) is one of these. Mossy chitons sport a ring of stiff bristles around their girdle. They prefer habitats that are a bit less exposed—for example, preferring tidepools over more exposed vertical rock faces. Mossy chitons stay put during the day, moving only at night and only when covered by the tide, typically returning "home" at the end of their nighttime feeding forays. They feed on algae and even small invertebrates, using their toothy radula to scrape food from rocky substrates.

Some of the invertebrates here and throughout the world feature color polymorphism—individuals within a single population colored differently from one another. The existence of color polymorphism is an interesting puzzle: Why do different color forms persist? Is being a different color than your neighbor an advantage?

Some color polymorphisms may indeed confer an ecological advantage. For example, on a hot, sunny day, animals with light-colored shells will heat up more slowly than their dark-colored counterparts, thereby gaining a bit of protection from the heat. In other cases, individuals with colors that are more difficult for a predator to see might be spared from predation compared with their more visible neighbors. And in some cases, color polymorphism remains a mystery: for example, the bright orange and purple coloration of the ochre sea star (see Species of Interest on the Rocky Northern Coast in chapter 4, Washington's Outer Coast) is unexplained.

But here's the most interesting bit: for such a polymorphism to persist, any ecological advantage it confers is confined to temporary situations in a dynamic world. If it were *always* an advantage to have a light-colored shell, for example, natural selection would quickly favor the lighter form over any other color. Thus, after a few generations, the entire population would have light-colored shells, and all other morphs would be lost. So to ecologists, persistent diversity in color and other traits is like a neon sign advertising traits subject to real-world trade-offs. Under some conditions,

The shells of the predatory dog whelk (*Nucella* sp.) exhibit color polymorphism, varying from black and brown to bright orange. Some evidence suggests that color polymorphism in this species has a genetic basis.

each morph must be favorable (or at least not harmful), or else it wouldn't still be present in the population.

Oregon Dunes

Nearly half of the Oregon coast is sandy beach, but the Oregon Dunes National Recreation Area deserves special notice. This fifty-four-mile-long complex of sand dunes that stretches from just north of Florence to Cape Arago, just south of Coos Bay, is the largest set of dunes along the West Coast. Florence itself sits within the dunes, a curious choice of urban planning but a testament to the draw of sand and sea.

Dunes form when sand blows inland from the beach. Here, prevailing winds from the west and an ample supply of dry sand have built the dunes over millennia, helped along by changes in sea level. Many of these waves of sand were formed long before the last ice age, and some have risen to more than 200 feet tall.

Open, shifting sands create a landscape that seems alive. The persistent wind tends to cover tracks in the sand, the transient evidence of human

European beach grass (*Ammophila arenaria*) is a stabilizing force on dunes, halting the flow of sand in an environment historically characterized by the dynamics of that sand.

presence as well as that of foxes, weasels, porcupines, and any number of others. Behind the high foredune fronting the beach, a lower-lying area features sizable lakes and more vegetation, with fingers of sand reaching into the foothill forests beyond.

Those high foredunes running parallel to the sea are relatively new features in this ancient landscape. In the mid-twentieth century, the US Forest Service widely planted an invasive beach grass (*Ammophila arenaria*), aiming to stem the inland flow of sand and keep the beach separate from the neighboring roads, campgrounds, and towns. This worked as planned; the beach grass, native to beaches of North Africa and Europe, rapidly stabilizes active dunes with belowground shoots that can grow more than six feet in six months. Of course, stabilizing the foredune has robbed the more inland areas of their supply of wind-driven sand from the beach—this was the point of planting in the first place—and started an ongoing parade of other early-colonizing plants that can quickly turn dunes into a forest. The result is a shrinking set of Oregon dunes.

SEA FOAM

Aphrodite, goddess of love and beauty, was born out of sea foam according to one version of classical Greek mythology. While it's admittedly difficult to imagine a fully formed goddess arising out of shoreline froth, sea foam nevertheless commands the attention of curious visitors, inspiring young and old alike to wonder: what exactly is it?

Like any foam, sea foam is pockets of gas trapped in a matrix—in this case, seawater. But water alone won't sustain the durable bubbles that lasting foam demands. In general, a mix of fats, proteins, and perhaps other solids dissolved in water fortify the bubbles and preserve their structure. Whipped cream, after all, requires the fat and protein of the cream in order to hold its form.

In the case of sea foam, the required dissolved materials are also fats and proteins, along with lignins, the long-chained molecules that lend strength to wood and are present in some

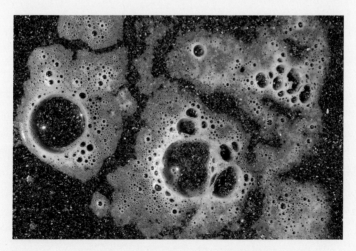

Vigorous churning transforms natural foaming agents into sea foam.

algae. And broken-down algae are indeed the source of these dissolved compounds in seawater, particularly in the aftermath of a bloom of single-celled algae offshore. The churning and turbulent mixing of water onshore then whips air into the mix of water and dissolved materials, creating foam, which can persist for hours or even days.

Sea foam isn't simply an inert product of physics but, rather, hosts all manner of life during its ephemeral existence. Diatoms and various bacteria, in particular, can make a home in its rafts, and invertebrates such as small crustaceans actually eat the foam, making a living from the decomposed materials of which it is made.

The right conditions—high winds while ample dissolved organic matter is in the water—can create huge volumes of foam. In at least one case, this has proved fatal to humans: five surfers drowned off the coast of the Netherlands in spring 2020 when thick layers of foam not only proved hazardous but also hampered rescue efforts.

Cape Arago

Cape Arago boasts three state parks, each of which offers something a little different. Sunset Bay State Park is a wide sandy beach with accessible but well-trampled tidepools. A bit farther south is Shore Acres State Park, the former estate of a timber baron, which affords an outstanding display of the local shoreline geology. And at the southern end of the road, Cape Arago State Park provides good access to a rich intertidal of mixed rock and sand. By virtue of surrounding landforms, the shorelines of both Sunset Bay and Cape Arago State Parks are protected from the strongest waves, and this is reflected in the ecological communities here.

Different from the volcanic rock that forms most of Oregon's head-lands to the north, Cape Arago is sedimentary rock. Throughout the area,

South Cove at Cape Arago State Park teems with intertidal life.

layers of sediment deposited over geologic time have been compressed and then tilted by tectonic forces to produce landforms that look vaguely like a giant layer cake turned on its side, evidence of the tectonic forces at work along this stretch of coastline.

For example, surrounding Cape Arago's Sunset Beach, the flat-topped cliffs mark the sea level at different points in recent earth history. The level on which the lighthouse sits was the seashore about 80,000 years ago; its current altitude is a compromise between changes in sea level and tectonic uplift since that time (see Tectonics and Subduction in chapter 1, The Tumultuous Earth). In between ice ages—or as a product of human-induced climate warming in the present day—sea level rises as ice on land melts and flows into the ocean, increasing its volume. As the seas rise, they flood coastlines. Waves crash onto the land and level it out, creating terraces. As sea level rises and falls against a background of tectonic uplift, it creates terraces at different levels. In the region of Cape

Arago, there are at least five distinct terraces, reflecting the sea level at different points in time. And because our present sea level is about as high as it has ever been in recent geological time, today's cliffs represent a temporary victory of uplift over erosion.

From the perspective of invertebrates and seaweeds, rock type matters. Different rock types heat and cool differently, have varying hardness, fracture differently, and are differentially likely to form pools or boulders or other structural elements of intertidal habitat. These characteristics influence habitat quality for invertebrates and seaweeds. For example, soft sedimentary rocks like those at Cape Arago may be attractive to boring clams but may be too soft and too easily eroded to support long-lived seaweeds. Rocky substrates that fracture easily may create cracks and crevices that become good homes and hiding places for small invertebrates. Large boulders can offer shade during daytime low tides, and tidepools offer refuge from desiccation.

Like many of the beaches along this stretch of coast, the rocky intertidal habitat here is shaped by sand, and the organisms found here tend to tolerate sand burial, at least for short periods. One of these is a kelp (*Laminaria setchellii*) that can live two decades or more. Its stiff stipe, equivalent to the trunk of a small tree, is perennial and strong enough to support the weight of the blade even in air—that is, these kelps stand up even when the tide is out. The stipes are bare in winter, having shed their blades to reduce the drag forces created by large waves, in much the same way that some trees shed their leaves to reduce the effects of winter wind and snow. New blades emerge from the tip of the stipe each spring. A peculiar species of limpet (*Lottia instabilis*) lives exclusively on *Laminaria* stipes, its shell conforming to the round stipe, making it easily distinguishable from its rock-dwelling flat relatives.

Halosaccion glandiforme (the genus name means "salt sac" and the species name means "shaped like an acorn") is classified as a red seaweed, but quite often it loses its red appearance and takes on a yellowish or golden color. It's common along much of the West Coast in exposed rocky intertidal habitats. Although relatives of this seaweed are flat red blades—for example, *Palmaria* (see Cattle Point Area, San Juan Island, in

Signs of life: despite their sandy surroundings, these long-lived subtidal kelps (*Laminaria setchellii*) hold fast to low rocks. Their bright golden blades signal new spring growth. Here, the kelp shares space with surfgrass (*Phyllospadix* sp.), which has similar habitat preferences.

chapter 3, Washington's Puget Sound and Greater Salish Sea)–*Halosaccion* has adopted a torpedo-like morphology that helps it tolerate conditions in the intertidal. The sacs are filled with seawater plus a little bit of gas, helping to reduce the stress of warm temperatures and desiccation during low tides and perhaps reducing drag forces when the seaweed is submerged. *Halosaccion* sometimes grows in great profusion, creating swathes of gold in rocky intertidal areas.

The relatively large black turban snail (*Tegula funebralis*) grows to be an inch or so in diameter and is common on rocky shores, where it can occur at very high densities. It likes to eat *Halosaccion* and also has a penchant for kelp species such as bull kelp (see Species of Interest in chapter 3) and giant kelp (*Macrocystis pyrifera*) when those kelps wash up on shore. This marine snail grows to be quite old: individuals can

Hitchhikers—here, tiny pale barnacles and a brown limpet—find a home on the back of a black turban snail (*Tegula funebralis*). The black snail sits amid the "salt sac" seaweed (*Halosaccion glandiforme*), conveniently one of the snail's preferred foods. *Halosaccion* can tolerate intertidal conditions, in part, by keeping its own supply of moisture handy.

certainly live to thirty years and, by some estimates, up to eighty to one hundred years. In snail terms, turban snails are sprinters: when faced with a predator, the turban snail can turn and escape at speeds of up to three inches per minute. That's impressive speed for a snail that could be a hundred years old.

The shells of black turban snails attract hitchhikers, often small barnacles but sometimes other snails—for example, the small black limpet (*Lottia asmi*), which itself is a type of snail although its shape differs from the coiled shells of its relatives. The black limpet grazes on microalgae and tends to prefer to live on shells of turban snails over other species. Or you might find the hooked slippersnail (*Crepidula adunca*) on the back of a turban snail. The slippersnail fixes itself to its host for the entirety of its adult life and is unusual among marine snails because, instead of grazing using a tongue-like radula, it casts a mucous net to capture food particles from the water column.

A sculpin's-eye view of a tidepool reveals a swath of pink coralline algae (middle) against a background of colorful seaweeds and seagrass, while a giant green anemone (*Anthopleura xanthogrammica*) waits for prey to happen by.

SIMPSON REEF

Immediately north of Cape Arago State Park's North Cove, the high vantage point of Simpson Reef Overlook offers a striking counterpoint to the low intertidal of Cape Arago's South Cove. Part of the Oregon Islands National Wildlife Refuge, this overlook offers an excellent place to see and hear a diversity of marine mammals. The reef itself, offshore between Shore Acres and Cape Arago State Parks, is a series of exposed rocks and islets, with Shell Island being the largest. Hauled out on these rocks, or foraging in the surrounding waters, are harbor seals, northern elephant seals, California sea lions, and Steller sea lions.

With luck and a pair of binoculars or spotting scope, visitors can spy whales offshore. Migrating gray whales appear seasonally, as do resident gray whales, a group that remains along the Oregon coast to feed in summer and fall. Occasionally, blue whales and orcas pass by. And thousands of Pacific loons stream by in the spring on their annual northward migration.

GRAY WHALE MIGRATION

Everything about large whales seems out of scale: eyeballs the diameter of dinner plates, tails like garage doors. But the annual commute of the gray whale (*Eschrichtius robustus*) belongs to a different rank altogether, the animals traversing the northern hemisphere as if going to the grocery store. And in a way, this is precisely what they are doing.

Food and heat and other resources aren't spread evenly across the globe; they're patchy. Gray whales take advantage of their size and speed to skip from one good patch to another, seasonally. In summer, they eat where the eating is good, in the productive waters of Alaska. They then head south along the West Coast to the warm, protected waters of Mexico to give birth and wait out the winter.

Nearly 30,000 animals make this 12,000-mile round-trip each year. On the way north in early spring, newborn calves do their best to keep up and gain weight fast, nursing 475 gallons of milk per day from patches on their mothers' skin. The milk itself is around 53 percent milk fat, thirteen times as rich as cow's milk, and comes out thick as toothpaste in the cold waters of the Pacific.

The whales tend to stay near the coast on their way northward with the new calves, protecting them from orcas and other predators. March and April, then, is the best time to see them from shore, as they make one of the longest commutes on the planet.

SOUTH SLOUGH

A slough is a creek that flows into a bay and is dominated by tidewater, creating a very sheltered, soft-sediment environment. A visit to the South Slough National Estuarine Reserve, which separates Cape Arago from the mainland near the mouth of Coos Bay, therefore offers an entirely

Simpson Reef provides habitat for a variety of sea life; seals and sea lions often are seen resting on the exposed rocks.

different experience of the rocky intertidal in this region's outer shore. The reserve, which occupies nearly 6,000 acres of natural area, is part of the National Estuarine Research Reserve system.

In sharp contrast to the exposed, high-energy sites typical of Cape Arago, the South Slough reserve has protected, low-energy sites shaped by the dual influences of salt water from the surrounding marine environment and freshwater entering from streams and rivers. A walk along trails through forested uplands brings visitors to the shore, with views of salt marshes, small islands, and open water beyond. The habitat supports a rich diversity of species, including salmon, eagles, great blue herons, oysters, and crabs, plus marsh grasses and mud-dwelling invertebrates such as clams and worms of many types.

Cape Blanco

The westernmost point in Oregon, Cape Blanco is—like Cape Arago—a prominent headland shaved flat by the oncoming surf before being lifted into its current position about 80,000 years ago. The cape itself is in the process of becoming a sea stack, as erosion produces landslides on either side of the current-day access road. The wind can be fierce here, making the power lines sing when conditions are just right. Perhaps this is a suitable place to recall Marcus Aurelius: "Be like the promontory against which the waves continually break, but it stands firm and tames the fury of the water around it." In the short term the rocks win, but in the fullness of time, even Aurelius's promontory cedes to the waves.

This spot is roughly the geological line at which Oregon becomes California. The political boundary between the states is, of course, about seventy miles south of the cape, and there is still plenty of sand south of Cape Blanco. But south of this point, geological Oregon begins to give way to the older rock of northern California, and the southern Oregon coast shows the influence of California's Klamath River. The sea-surface currents shift too, becoming more organized and pushing generally

Cape Blanco, Oregon's westernmost land feature, boasts the state's oldest standing lighthouse, built in 1870.

southward along the coast, transporting spores, larvae, and juveniles of many species in the process.

The north side of Cape Blanco features particularly good rocky intertidal habitat, with small boulders closer to the beach and larger rocks and benches nearest the cape itself. Trails lead down to the beach from an unpaved parking lot west of the lighthouse. The rocky habitat emerges from sand and driftwood as low tide exposes a diversity of substrates, from small cobbles to large boulders. The greatest diversity of life here, as elsewhere, is likely to be woven among the larger rocks, which are more stable and not constantly disturbed by breaking waves.

The habitat here supports a classic rocky-intertidal species assemblage that brings together many of the species and subhabitats seen along the southern Oregon coast. Cape Blanco features what may be a happy intermediate oceanographic regime, reflecting a transition between higher levels of invertebrate recruitment and growth to the north and lower levels to the south. And as elsewhere, the gooseneck barnacles here tell us the site experiences substantial wave action, which is probably not surprising for a rocky headland with a lighthouse.

Among the high and mid intertidal rocks scuttle two species of shore crab common along the West Coast: the purple shore crab (*Hemigrapsus nudus*) with spotted claws and the lined shore crab (*Pachygrapsus crassipes*) with black and green lines. Both are scavengers and eat much of whatever they can find, but they rely mainly on algae.

Other small crabs abound here, too. Juvenile Dungeness crabs and their close relatives (*Metacarcinus* and *Cancer* spp.) hide under medium-sized rocks in the lower intertidal, while kelp crabs (*Pugettia* spp.) are often visibly on patrol. And then there's the black-clawed crab (*Lophopanopeus bellus*), about two inches wide with a curiously muscular appearance.

The arrestingly flat porcelain crab (*Petrolisthes cinctipes*) isn't a true crab—like hermit crabs, it has only three pairs of walking legs, rather than the four of true crabs—but it is nevertheless very crab-like and can be found in great densities under intertidal rocks. More impressive, though, is its ability to drop legs as an escape mechanism, growing them back within weeks.

In the mid intertidal pools that sit among stable rock benches, several species of hermit crabs and olive shells live among the urchins and anemones. And here dwells a snail with a fierce name: the dire whelk (*Lirabuccinum dirum*, formerly *Searlesia dira*). The snail's heavy shell protects it from crabs while it stalks all kinds of prey, from chitons to worms and mussels, although its predilection for scavenging dead animals somewhat undercuts its reputation as a predator. The dire whelk attaches its vase-shaped yellowish egg capsules to hard surfaces; from these hatch tiny snails, off to seek their fortunes. Beautiful top snails (*Calliostoma* spp.) adorn pools here, and keyhole limpets cling to the boulders.

A common intertidal snail, with a pointed shell, the dire whelk (*Lirabuccinum dirum*) is both a predator on other invertebrates and a scavenger; here, dire whelks (three at center) feed on a larger black turban snail (*Tegula funebralis*).

The blue top snail (*Calliostoma ligatum*) is commonly found on kelp and other brown algae, which are favored foods. It will reportedly crawl quickly away from approaching sea stars.

Harris Beach

Located at the northern edge of the town of Brookings, Oregon's south-westernmost outpost, Harris State Beach is a gem. It offers soft sand, tidepools, sea stacks, arches, and a large offshore island that is home to nesting seabirds. Stormy in winter, intermittently sunny and foggy in summer, its variation in weather is matched by the variation in habitats. The sand, too, comes and goes seasonally: rock pools full of sand in the summer may empty out with winter waves.

Occasional warm, dry winds blow seaward from the Coast Range down the valley of the Chetco River, making Brookings noticeably warmer than elsewhere along this coast; in fact, temperatures can be in the high 70s during the winter. The "Brookings Effect" is a quirk of climate that likely helps shape the intertidal communities here.

In summer, Harris Beach's hard intertidal surfaces are covered in kelps, red algae, and surfgrass, even as the rocks to which they are attached are enveloped by sand. The vegetable matter can become so dense that it's difficult to walk among the pools, but the species hiding underneath all that seaweed are worth seeking out. Given the shade and protection at hand, the underlying assemblage of species is one visitors might find elsewhere in a cave or under a rocky overhang. There are many tunicates of both colonial and solitary forms, bryozoans, and a few sponges.

Higher up, the top snails of Cape Blanco are gone, but the black turban snails (*Tegula* spp.) remain, some of them a marker of the site's dynamics: *Tegula* species can live many years, and where they survive long enough to become large, this is an indicator of favorable longer-term conditions at the site.

Creeping among the rather dull seaweeds are brightly colored nudibranchs. Nudibranchs are shell-less snails that take a range of forms and colors; they are one of several related groups known commonly as sea slugs. Lacking shells for protection, some nudibranchs harbor stinging cells to deter predators and are often brightly colored to deter predators.

Just offshore lies Goat Island (also sometimes called Bird Island). At twenty-one acres, this is the largest offshore island in Oregon, and in 1936 it was designated as part of the Oregon Islands National Wildlife Refuge.

The brooding anemone (*Epiactis prolifera*) is unusual in at least two ways: First, it broods its young, so that the small adult (one to two inches across) sports minuscule pale juvenile anemones on its orange stalk, as seen here. Second, all individuals of this species begin life as females, developing over time into hermaphrodites with two different sets of reproductive organs.

The leather star (*Dermasterias imbricata*) shelters among damp vegetation at low tide. Apart from having a distinctive texture and appearance, these stars produce a subtle odor that some people find comparable to garlic. Urchins, too, can sense this predator and quickly escape when it approaches.

In spring and summer some 100,000 seabirds nest on the island, about 5,000 birds per acre—crowded conditions indeed. The island has relatively deep soil that lends itself to seabirds that nest in burrows, including Leach's storm petrel and tufted puffins (see Birds of the Exposed Coast in chapter 5, The Northern Oregon Coast). Marine mammals (see Species of Interest, below), including seals, sea lions, and whales, all congregate offshore.

From the perspective of invertebrates and seaweeds, the rocky landforms here are habitable islands amid a sea of sand. Space for settlement

A large rock set in a sea of sand shows clear intertidal zonation, in which the sea stars do not eat the sand-tolerant anemones (lower on the rock); instead, the stars eat the mussels, which restricts the mussels to the upper parts of the rock. The stars cannot move well when out of the water and also are more vulnerable to bird predators when exposed to air; hence, they cannot dominate the upper reaches of the intertidal environment. As a consequence, the sharp boundary between the mussel community (upper part of the rock) and the lower anemone community is a dynamic compromise of both physical and biological processes.

and growth here is limited by the amount of rock, and much of the hard substrate that does exist is nearly vertical, further compressing suitable intertidal habitat. Dynamic sands regularly uncover bare rock, opening space and offering organisms a place to settle, but these spots are prone to scouring and can quickly become buried as sands move over time. Evidence of shifting sand is everywhere here.

SPECIES OF INTEREST
Coralline Algae
Pink may not be a color we immediately associate with intertidal habitats, but on closer inspection, it's seemingly everywhere on rocky shores.

What might at first appear to be bushy pink tufts or pale pink coatings on rock or shells are in fact coralline algae, seaweeds of many genera and species. Found growing in tidepools and elsewhere along the West Coast, coralline algae occupy both shallow and deep habitats all over the world.

A special group of red algae that have calcareous deposits in their cell walls, coralline algae are distinguished from other red algae by their pinkish color and hard skeleton, a stony exterior that comes from the calcareous deposits contained within their cell walls. Because of their stony exoskeletons, coralline algae tolerate a moderate amount of disturbance, including sand scour and wave action. They take two primary growth forms: One is flat and encrusting, adhering tightly to rock and other solid substrates and sometimes looking like pink paint splashed on rocks or shells. The other is upright and bushy with jointed branches that can bend with wave action. The genus *Calliarthron* is an example of one of the bushy forms, but other species of both bushy and crustose forms are common.

Encrusting forms of coralline algae sometimes cover the shells of limpets and snails, perhaps affording them a bit of protection from their visual predators. For example, the shell of the whitecap limpet (*Acmaea mitra*) is bright white, but living individuals typically are covered by pink encrusting coralline algae—the same alga that makes up their primary food source. Covered in pink, these limpets blend in with their food source and, perhaps relatedly, are among the few local limpet species that don't appear to mount a protective response against predators.

Coralline algae tend to be more resistant to grazing than many of the fleshy algae, but they can be easily overgrown by faster-growing seaweeds and invertebrates. Only a handful of specialized grazers favor coralline algae as food, and those that do tend to have hardened mouthparts that can handle the stony exterior—among these are a few species of chitons and limpets, including the aforementioned whitecap limpet. Other invertebrates make use of crustose corallines in a very different way: the larvae of some species such as abalone choose these algae as a place to settle and grow, cued by chemicals emitted by the alga or its bacterial associates that indicate a favorable habitat.

Pink coralline algae are colorful and common on the West Coast, durable primary producers thanks to their manufacture of hard shell-like material. They come in numerous shapes and sizes, including (left) crustose—here, on the shell of a whitecap limpet (*Acmaea mitra*)—and (below) branching, or articulated, forms such as the genus *Calliarthron*.

Tar Spot Algae

In rocky intertidal places all along the southern Oregon coast is a blackish crust that looks like tar, but instead of tar, this is a type of red seaweed known as Petrocelis—and it's obvious why its common name is tar spot. Petrocelis at one time was thought to spend its entire life as a crust, but now we know that it's the alternate life stage of *Mastocarpus*, an upright, branching red seaweed that typically is found growing nearby. The spores produced by Petrocelis settle and grow into blades of *Mastocarpus*, which, after a few complicated steps, produce spores that grow into new crusts of Petrocelis.

The feather boa kelp (*Egregia menziesii*) has strap-like long fronds covered with small blades and air bladders. The morphology of *Egregia* can vary with wave energy and age, producing a range of forms.

Feather Boa Kelp

The feather boa kelp (*Egregia menziesii*) is found in low intertidal areas all along the southern Oregon coast. Though big and brown like other kelps, it has a distinctive shape, with strap-like long fronds covered with small blades, and it's certainly the only kelp species that can be mistaken for a feather boa. Small air-filled sacs called pneumatocysts are scattered along the fronds to add buoyancy. *Egregia* is conspicuous among the low intertidal seaweeds not only because of its shape but also its large size: fronds can grow to be several yards long. One species of limpet (*Discurria incessa*, formerly *Lottia incessa*) lives only on *Egregia*, where it rambles up and down the long, flat frond, grazing as it goes. It eats both the kelp itself as well as smaller algal species growing on the kelp.

Giant Green Anemone

Ubiquitous along the coast's rocky shorelines is the giant green anemone (*Anthopleura xanthogrammica*). When underwater, it unfurls its glowing

Long-lived and often gregarious, giant green anemones (*Anthopleura xanthogrammica*) feed on small fish, crabs, and detached mussels, among others.

bright-green tentacles around a broad oral disc. When out of the water on a low tide, it closes up into a muddy green lump, waiting for the water to come back. Exposed to the air at low tides, this species fastens shell fragments and small stones around its central column, presumably to reduce evaporation and exposure to ultraviolet radiation.

Photosynthetic microbes generally live within the tentacles of these anemones, contributing to their emerald color. Their tentacles are covered in explosive stinging cells that, when triggered, launch minute barbed projectiles into their prey. The projectiles are tethered to the anemones, allowing them to latch onto their prey and prevent their escape.

These brilliantly colored, photogenic anemones can live for many decades without discernible aging. Perhaps relatedly, they have a remarkable power to heal their own wounds and regenerate body parts, including tentacles and even the central oral disc. They also make at least two kinds of sunscreen with which they protect themselves; one of these—green fluorescent protein—is responsible for their coloration and it is the same protein that laboratories worldwide use for all kinds of molecular assays.

Nudibranchs

One of the greatest delights when poking around the intertidal is coming across a nudibranch. Many are brightly colored and showy, while others blend into their backgrounds so well that they can't be spotted without concerted effort. Finding a nudibranch in the wild feels like discovering a gemstone, even though they are common the world over. At least 170 species are known from along the Pacific coast.

Unlike snails, which tend to have protective shells, nudibranchs lack such protection beyond their larval stages (hence *nudi*, meaning "nude"). So they need a defensive strategy to avoid being eaten, and for the most part, they depend on chemistry. Those that are colorful may be advertising their toxic defensive compounds. Some species pull off an impressive feat of thievery: after eating hydrozoans, which are relatives of jellyfish and anemones, they steal their prey's stinging cells and store them in the appendages on their backs, converting food into weaponry.

Even though nudibranchs are soft-bodied and may appear intricately delicate, they are all predators, eating mainly stationary prey like hydrozoans, bryozoans, sponges, and anemones, although in some cases they

The bright coloration of some sea slugs (here, the nudibranch *Janolus fuscus*) is a warning sign to predators.

may eat other sea slugs. And all are hermaphrodites, so that a mating encounter is likely to leave both partners inseminated. The slugs then deposit eggs clustered together in a sticky ribbon of sorts.

Mussels

Wherever there is a solid surface along the West Coast, you'll likely find mussels between the high- and low-tide lines. Mussels are bivalves, having two shells that join at a hinge, a characteristic they share with clams and oysters. Unlike most other bivalves, however, mussels secure themselves to the substrate by making byssal threads—strong, elastic, protein-based filaments that withstand both wet and dry conditions—which makes life possible for them in the challenging conditions of the intertidal zone. Mussels eat by filtering water onto a mucous sheet covering their gills, of all things; the gills then help to pull the sheet into the mussel's mouth.

Along the exposed outer coast, the California mussel (*Mytilus californianus*) is most common. This is the largest and most robust mussel on the West Coast, growing to eight inches long and having a blue tint underlying its dark outer covering. It is a favorite food of the ochre sea star (see Species of Interest on the Rocky Northern Coast in chapter 4, Washington's Outer Coast), but it has also fed humans for thousands of years.

In more protected bays and estuaries, the smaller and smoother Pacific blue mussel (*M. trossulus*) takes over. But here is where things get complicated: the Mediterranean mussel (*M. galloprovincialis*), introduced to the US West Coast from Europe and cultivated commercially, looks quite similar to the native Pacific blue mussel. And a third species, the common blue mussel (*M. edulis*), often served in seafood dishes, is also thought to be introduced and again looks similar and occupies the same habitats. Further confusing the matter, all three of these species can hybridize, so sorting them out takes more patience than a casual observer likely has, possibly requiring genetic analysis.

Mussels are good environmental sentinels. They accumulate chemical contaminants in their tissues, and these can be analyzed to estimate contaminant levels in surrounding waters. In addition to detecting more than a hundred pollutants monitored under the US Clean Water Act, mussel tissues can indicate public health trends by detecting, for example, caffeine—and even opioids and cocaine—near urban areas. Harmful algal blooms, too, can leave toxic domoic acid behind in mussel tissues.

Purple Olive Snail

The purple olive snail, or purple olivella (*Callianax biplicata*, formerly *Olivella biplicata*), is a sand-adapted species found in the intertidal to depths of more than a hundred feet. Their shells are smooth and shiny, with traces of purple and gray. Active at night when the tide is high, their wedge-shaped foot plows trails through the sand as they move about in search of food. They burrow into the sand as the tide recedes. Their predators include moon snails, which drill holes in the shell to get at the soft tissues inside, and sea stars, which can elicit an escape response: when olivellas sense the proximity of a sea star, they will quickly bury themselves in the sand. The beauty of the olivella shell has long been appreciated by Native Americans, who historically used them for trading;

Purple olive snails (*Callianax biplicata*, formerly *Olivella biplicata*), which typically burrow in sand during the day, here (center right) occupy a pool at low tide.

beads made from these shells dating back many thousands of years have been found in south-central Oregon and at other inland sites.

Gumboot Chiton

Rocky areas at Cape Arago and elsewhere along the coast are home to the gumboot chiton (*Cryptochiton stelleri*), the largest chiton in the world. It grows to about the size of a large boot, hence its name. Like other chitons, it sports eight wing-shaped plates along its back, but unlike other chitons, the plates are nearly entirely covered by the leathery thick reddish-brown mantle, giving rise to the animal's nickname "the wandering meatloaf." The teeth of all chitons are highly mineralized, making them very hard, but the teeth of gumboot chitons are truly special in that they contain a rare mineral previously known only from rocks. Gumboots live submerged most of the time, where they use gills to obtain oxygen from seawater, but when exposed at low tide, they can get oxygen from air. They tend to feed at night and take cover during the day. Given their large size, they are more easily dislodged from their rocky substrates than most other chitons, and hence you can often find them washed ashore after storms.

The gumboot chiton (*Cryptochiton stelleri*) is conspicuous because of its large size; it can be roughly the size and texture of a football. It is most often found clinging to rocky substrates. These chitons reportedly live forty years or more. Photo by P. Hunt.

Acorn Barnacle

Oh, the humble barnacle. Ubiquitous, cream-colored, and so bland that one might ask, Are they even alive? But the barnacle is a keyhole through which to glimpse the weird world of marine invertebrates, a great example of wonders hiding in plain sight. Charles Darwin recognized this, devoting two entire volumes to the creatures.

First, the basics: the acorn barnacle (*Balanus glandula*) is a crustacean inside a little hut it makes out of shell material. As they settle from the plankton, young barnacles glue themselves in place on hard surfaces in the intertidal, so that as adults they are permanently attached and oriented head-down. When immersed, they eat with their legs, which gracefully comb the water to entrain small particles and deliver the particles to the barnacle inside its shell.

Barnacles have outrageously long penises, generally multiple times the length of their bodies. Proportionately, these are likely the longest in the world. This fact makes them famous among biologists (granted, a limited sort of fame), but apart from mere trivia, the appendage hints at central questions of biology and ecology, telling us about where the animal can live and how it does so.

The acorn barnacle is hermaphroditic—having both male and female reproductive organs in the same individual—and fertilization happens internally. That is, one barnacle must deliver sperm to another barnacle's eggs in order to reproduce. Given that adult barnacles are stuck in place for life, how might they accomplish this reproductive feat? A long-reaching delivery system, that's how. And so two barnacles can fertilize each others' eggs, so long as they are less than a penis-length away from one another. The thin penis snakes in between the closed plates of its intended mate to fertilize the internal eggs.

The great densities and clumped distribution of barnacles are a necessary side effect of this mode of reproduction. Think about it: have you ever seen just *one* barnacle? The species needs dense aggregations to reproduce, and sparse barnacles are lonely indeed. Sometimes acorn barnacles take this to an extreme: where space is limiting, acorn barnacles can become tall and skinny, forming dense hummocks (see chapter 5, The Northern Oregon Coast).

Finally, barnacles advertise conditions along the coast. For example, the dimensions of their feeding legs and penis will vary with the flow rate of the surrounding water. They can live out of water for hours, but not indefinitely, and so they can't live too far above the higher high-tide line. And because predatory snails eat them (barnacles can't run away, being glued in place) at lower tidal heights, they are restricted to a defined band along the shore (see Intertidal Zonation in chapter 2, Living between the Tides).

Other barnacles are showier, perhaps—for example, softball-sized subtidal species or gooseneck barnacles (see Species of Interest on the Rocky Northern Coast in chapter 4, Washington's Outer Coast) on leathery stalks or those that somehow colonize and ride upon passing whales. But the acorn barnacle has much to teach us.

Intertidal Fishes

Intertidal habitats are full of fishes, though it may not seem so at low tide. As the tide flows out, fishes move out with it, or they remain submerged and hidden in rock pools to avoid desiccation. As the tide flows back in, intertidal fishes return to feed, mainly on invertebrates. Several fish species are common in intertidal areas along the West Coast.

SHINER SURFPERCH

Flashing, darting, and schooling, shiner surfperch (*Cymatogaster aggregata*) grow to a few inches in length and are common in eelgrass beds and other sheltered habitats. Unusually for fishes, they give birth to live young. Many larger animals, from halibut to seals to eagles, make a meal of them.

NORTHERN CLINGFISH

The small northern clingfish (*Gobiesox meandricus*) hangs out under—or, rather, directly on—low boulders in the intertidal. Their pectoral fins form

The northern clingfish (*Gobiesox meandricus*), stuck to a rock, is not dangerous but can appear ill-tempered in photographs.

a suction cup, giving them a very strong grip with which to hang onto the rock and maintain position despite surging water. Juveniles may develop on bull kelp (see Species of Interest in chapter 3, Washington's Puget Sound and Greater Salish Sea) before moving to more permanent homes along the shore.

SCULPINS

The Cottidae family of fishes commonly live in and among rocky inter-tidal pools, zooming clandestinely around in impressive camouflage and making it difficult to distinguish among individual species. Befitting their lifestyles in small pools, most grow to only a few inches, although a few larger species tend to live in deeper water. They may eat algae or amphipods, copepods, and small worms.

PRICKLEBACKS

These fishes in the family Stichaeidae aren't true eels but are certainly eel-like, with tapered long bodies and often trivially small pectoral fins. Four species are common in the Pacific Northwest, found among cobbles

A sculpin (family Cottidae) hides in a tidepool among pink coralline algae.

and under more substantial rocks along the shore. The largest of these, the monkeyface prickleback (*Cebidichthys violaceus*), can be more than two feet long, although smaller individuals are more common among intertidal rocks.

HERRING

Foot-long fish, herring (*Clupea pallasi*) form massive schools, even in shallow waters. These fish typically aren't seen from intertidal vantage points, but in springtime their eggs (roe) can positively cover kelp, rocks, and other stationary surfaces in the nearshore. In areas crowded with spawning herring, the egg masses can be an inch or two thick, rendering the substrate unrecognizable and transforming the shallows into a milky buffet for fish, marine mammals, and humans. Indeed, harvesting roe on kelp continues to be an important commercial and subsistence activity in British Columbia, Alaska, and elsewhere.

SURF SMELT

Coastal visitors might be treated to the sight of surf smelt (*Hypomesus pretiosus*) spawning in the upper few inches of water on coarse-grained sandy beaches, in broad daylight. They seem to prefer to spawn in the afternoon, at high tide on beaches with some degree of freshwater input. Spawning happens year-round but only occasionally, ranging from many beaches in the greater Salish Sea and on coarse-sand beaches along the outer coasts of Washington and Oregon. The tiny eggs are adhesive, sticking to beach particles, where they incubate for several weeks before hatching. As with herring spawning aggregations, surf smelt can be a bonanza for salmon and marine mammals, which eat them enthusiastically.

BAT RAY AND BIG SKATE

Although bat rays (*Myliobatis californica*) and big skates (*Raja binoculata*) are unlikely to be seen from the beach, their presence can be indicated by what they leave behind. Low tide in soft-sediment habitats often reveals somewhat-mysterious shallow, circular pits. These are the results of skates and rays foraging in the mud at high tide, searching for clams and crustaceans and other tasty infauna that they crush and grind with oddly flattened teeth. Skates and rays have mouths on their undersides well below their snouts, and when they feed, the effect is rather like a flying saucer landing on a mudflat and flapping around to expose and capture prey, creating the pits visible at low tide.

Marine Mammals

Marine mammals seem to captivate people more than any other denizen of the sea. Sure, their large eyes and curious, often playful behaviors help. But more fundamentally, we seem to recognize a connection to these fellow mammals—warm-blooded and air-breathing—that have somehow invaded the saltwater world. (Or, more precisely: *re*invaded, since animal life first arose in the sea, far back in geological time.) It is as if your pet dog had taken up hunting for squid while free diving and, in the process, easily eclipsed all human records for breath holding and depth.

Appreciation for marine mammals is so widespread that the US has a law specifically protecting them, creatively entitled the Marine Mammal Protection Act (MMPA) of 1972. Most species have increased in population size since the protections have been in place. It remains a thrill to see marine mammals in the wild as they move with fluid grace and power through what is, to us, a foreign medium.

These mammals fall into four broad categories, three of which are represented along the West Coast: whales and dolphins (Cetacea), seals and sea lions (Pinnipedia), and otters, which are in the weasel family. The fourth category includes manatees and dugongs, the only North Pacific species of which, the Steller's sea cow, was hunted to extinction in the eighteenth century. (Of bureaucratic interest: the polar bear is also legally a marine mammal in the US, but we omit it here, because it is exclusively Arctic—and also because it is a bear.)

Being warm-blooded in a cold ocean means burning a *lot* of calories. A Steller sea lion needs about ten times as much energy as an adult human does every day, and large whales require hundreds of times what we do. And because West Coast marine mammals get these calories by eating other animals—in the case of some orcas, that means eating other mammals—they can have a big impact on the environments of which they are a part. Gray whales, for example, stir up literally tons of sediment when they feed along the seafloor, sucking down fish, crustaceans, and other animals living in and on the mud. The resulting mud plumes are visible from the air, and seabirds including the endangered marbled murrelet dive into them, feeding on invertebrates the whales miss. Suspended nutrients then fertilize the sunlit waters at the surface, triggering a bloom of new life.

Similarly, a single sea otter can clean out a small bay's worth of abalone or urchins; the return of otters to a region can flip the local ecosystem from urchin-dominated to kelp-dominated, with cascading ecological effects, and the loss of sea otters can do the opposite. In sum, mammals, perhaps more than most other species, tend to change the world around them.

WHALES AND DOLPHINS

Whales and dolphins are divided into two groups: those with teeth and those with baleen (plates of a hard fingernail-like substance through which food is filtered). The toothed whales include dolphins, and the most common of these in the Pacific Northwest are two species of porpoises

(Dall's and harbor), along with the dolphins: orcas (see Species of Interest in chapter 3, Washington's Puget Sound and Greater Salish Sea), Pacific white-sided dolphins, short-finned pilot whales, and Risso's dolphins. The sperm whale is the largest of the toothed whales, and it may appear occasionally offshore in the Pacific Northwest but is not routinely present.

Baleen whales in Washington and Oregon are the minke (*Balaenoptera acutorostrata*), the humpback (*Megaptera novaeangliae*), and the California gray whale (*Eschrichtius robustus*). In the wake of the MMPA, the 1973 US Endangered Species Act (ESA), and the International Whaling Commission's moratorium on commercial whaling in 1986, populations of these and other large whales have generally been increasing. The West Coast gray whale population has not required protection under the ESA since 1994, and many West Coast humpback populations are similarly recovering. The MMPA, however, continues to protect all marine mammals from commercial harvest.

SEALS AND SEA LIONS

Seals and sea lions are distinct groups that are often conflated in the popular imagination. Technically, they are distinguished by the presence or absence of external ears—sea lions have them, seals don't—but, more practically, if it looks like a sausage wallowing around awkwardly on land, it's a seal; if it's more coordinated, using its flippers to move about, it's a sea lion.

The harbor seal (*Phoca vitulina*) is the region's most common marine mammal, occurring in coastal regions throughout the northern hemisphere. They often are seen hauled out of the cold water, usually on small islands, draped across boulders or sprawling on rocky benches.

The other member of the seal family that occurs in this region is the northern elephant seal (*Mirounga angustirostris*). It is relatively rare in these waters but memorable because of its large size. Humans very nearly hunted this species to extinction in the nineteenth century, and its population rebounded from a single tiny population in Mexico in the 1890s to more than 200,000 individuals in the early twenty-first century. Members of this species spend most of their lives at sea but come ashore

Harbor seals (*Phoca vitulina*) sun themselves on the low tide at Yaquina Head.

to breed and molt. The northernmost breeding population is in British Columbia on the Strait of Juan de Fuca, just across the strait from Port Angeles, Washington.

Sea lions in the Pacific Northwest include the California sea lion (*Zalophus californianus*) and the Steller sea lion (*Eumetopias jubatus*). The two can be distinguished by their size, with Stellers being by far the larger of the two, and by their vocalizations: California sea lions "bark," while Steller sea lions sound more like growling bears. Male California sea lions can be nearly eight feet long and weigh more than 700 pounds; male Stellers can be more than ten feet long and nearly 2,500 pounds. The larger Steller sea lions are distinguishable by their prominent snouts and (in mature males) large foreheads. The species is named not for the stars but for the eighteenth-century naturalist and explorer Georg Steller, whose name also graces the Steller's jay, the Steller's sea eagle, the extinct Steller's sea cow, and the gumboot chiton (*Cryptochiton stelleri*, earlier in Species of Interest), among other species.

While the California sea lion uses a range of accessible coastal sites to haul out, Stellers prefer more isolated island sites. Both can tolerate estuarine waters, which they occasionally enter to forage, and the California sea lion may venture far up rivers into fully freshwater. Indeed, these mammals have become a management challenge in the Columbia River, where they eat endangered salmon at the Bonneville Dam, more than 130 miles upriver from the mouth of the Columbia.

OTTERS

The sea otter (*Enhydra lutris*), famously saved from the brink of extinction in the twentieth century, was reintroduced to Washington's outer coast in 1969–70. The population has since grown to reasonable size, but the species remains restricted to a small area around Cape Flattery on Washington's outer coast. Although formerly common along Oregon's coast, the species is no longer established there.

More common in much of the Northwest is the North American river otter (*Lontra canadensis*), which can venture onto rocky shores and into both freshwater and salt water in search of food. It is quite possible to mistake a river otter for a sea otter while it is foraging in the marine environment. Up close, however, the two are easily distinguishable: sea otters are furrier and stubbier, with flippers rather than rear feet; river otters are narrow and lankier, with long tails and four feet that are all of about the same size. Like sea otters, river otters are members of the weasel family, and on land, river otters move much like their weasel cousins.

BEYOND THE NORTHWEST COAST

Harris Beach and the immediately surrounding area is the last stretch of easily accessible rocky intertidal habitat north of Patrick's Point, eighty-five miles to the south in California. It's a short jaunt south of Brookings, Oregon, to the state line and a corresponding change in ecological context. Upon entering California, the visitor encounters a transition area of wind and sand, with open vistas west of US Highway 101. Dunes of fine sand hide the sea from view in places, dune grass visibly stabilizes the shoreline, and beaches of smooth cobbles and larger sand grains lie alongside a system of coastal lagoons.

It's a fitting coda to the Oregon coast—and to the Northwest Coast as a whole. From the Strait of Juan de Fuca to Brookings is roughly 550 miles, a distance greater than from New York to North Carolina, encompassing long stretches of wild shorelines, the mouth of one of the continent's great rivers, and countless sea stacks, headlands, and pocket beaches. Land meets sea in ways that are by turns violent and torpid, with these extremes continually shaping the ecological communities of the intertidal zone.

Throughout, the patterns we notice in the living world demand explanations—or at least inquiries: *what lives where, and why?* The answers lie in some combination of biology and physics, geology and time, with adventures along the Northwest Coast offering surpassing illustrations of ecology in action.

Kelp and a sea star cling to the only hard surface in the sand.

ACKNOWLEDGMENTS

With deep gratitude, we thank the many people who have helped bring this story to life. Many colleagues, students, and associates have shared their knowledge with us over the years and have profoundly shaped these pages; we hope they see a reflection of themselves in this work. We are especially grateful to our editor, Andrew Berzanskis, and the team at UW Press for their expert guidance and to copyeditor Kris Fulsaas for her invaluable eye for detail, and to graphic designer Zoe Vartanian for her informative figures. We appreciate the comments of two anonymous reviewers and a handful of colleagues who generously loaned us photographs we could not have obtained otherwise.

FURTHER READING

Alt, David D., and Donald W. Hyndman. 1975. *Roadside Geology of Northern California*. Missoula, MT: Mountain Press.

Angell, Tony, and Kenneth C. Balcomb III. 1982. *Marine Birds and Mammals of Puget Sound*. Seattle: University of Washington Press.

Begon, M., J. L. Harper, C. R. Townsend et al. 1990. *Ecology: Individuals, Populations and Communities*. Brookline Village, MA: Blackwell Scientific Publications.

Carson, Rachel L. 1951. *The Sea Around Us*. Oxford, UK: Oxford University Press.

DeLella, Audrey, and Joseph Gaydos. 2015. *The Salish Sea: Jewel of the Pacific Northwest*. Seattle: Sasquatch Books.

Eschmeyer, William N., and Earl Stannard Herald. 1999. *A Field Guide to Pacific Coast Fishes: North America*. New York: Houghton Mifflin Harcourt.

Franklin, Jerry F., and C. T. Dyrness. 1988. *Natural Vegetation of Oregon and Washington*. Corvallis: Oregon State University Press.

Gaines, Steven D., and Mark W. Denny. 2007. *Encyclopedia of Tidepools and Rocky Shores*. Berkeley: University of California Press.

Garrison, Tom S. 2012. *Oceanography: An Invitation to Marine Science*. Belmont, CA: Cengage Learning.

Griggs, Gary B. 2010. *Introduction to California's Beaches and Coast*. Berkeley: University of California Press.

Iselin, Josie. 2019. *The Curious World of Seaweed*. Berkeley: Heyday.

Komar, Paul D. 1997. *The Pacific Northwest Coast: Living with the Shores of Oregon and Washington*. Durham, NC: Duke University Press.

Kozloff, Eugene N. 2000. *Seashore Life of the Northern Pacific Coast: An Illustrated Guide to Northern California, Oregon, Washington, and British Columbia*. Seattle: University of Washington Press.

Kruckeberg, Arthur R. 1995. *The Natural History of Puget Sound Country*. Seattle: University of Washington Press.

Lamb, Andrew, and Bernard P. Hanby. 2005. *Marine Life of the Pacific Northwest*. Madeira Park, BC: Harbour Publishing.

Love, Milton. n.d. *Probably More Than You Wanted to Know About the Fishes of the Pacific Coast*. Santa Barbara, CA: Really Big Press.

MacKinnon, Andrew, Jim Pojar, Paul B. Alaback et al. 2004. *Plants of the Pacific Northwest Coast*. Edmonton, AB: Lone Pine Publishing.

Madlener, Judith Cooper. 1977. *The Sea Vegetable Book*. New York: Clarkson N. Potter.

Miller, Marli Bryant. 2014. *Roadside Geology of Oregon*. Missoula, MT: Mountain Press.

Morris, Robert Harding, Donald Putnam Abbott, and Eugene Clinton Haderlie. 1980. *Intertidal Invertebrates of California*. Stanford, CA: Stanford University Press.

Ricketts, Edward F., Jack Calvin, Joel W. Hedgpeth, and David W. Phillips. 1985. *Between Pacific Tides*. Stanford, CA: Stanford University Press.

Schultz, Stewart T. 1990. *The Northwest Coast: A Natural History*. Portland, OR: Timber Press.

Sept, J. Duane. 2019. *The New Beachcomber's Guide to the Pacific Northwest*. Madeira Park, BC: Harbour Publishing.

Shugar, Dan H. 2015. *Geology Underfoot in Western Washington*. Seattle: University of Washington Press.

Steelquist, Robert. 2016. *The Northwest Coastal Explorer: Your Guide to the Places, Plants, and Animals of the Pacific Coast*. Portland, OR: Timber Press.

Strickland, Richard M. 1983. *The Fertile Fjord: Plankton in Puget Sound*. Seattle: University of Washington Press.

Wertheim, Anne. 2002. *The Intertidal Wilderness: A Photographic Journey through Pacific Coast Tidepools*. Berkeley: University of California Press.

INDEX

Page numbers in *italics* indicate photos or other illustrations

coastal ecosystems (*continued*)
geological context for, 21, 29-30, 139-40; habitat complexity in, 21, 29-30, 38; high- vs. low-energy environments, 41, 43; interspecies dynamics in, 49, 51-53, 55-61; invasive species in, *53-54*, 85, 158, 198, *198*; land-sea linkages in, 58, 59-60, 106-7, 122, 124, 144; primary production in, 44-46; salinity variations in, 39-40, 133, *133*, 156-57; sea stars as keystone species, 132; species assemblages and diversity in, 21, 23, 30, 35, 41, 61-62, 132; temperature variation and microclimates, 37-38, 156-57; tidal cycles and their impacts, 35-37, *36*, 63. *See also* biological productivity; coastal geology; habitat types and variants; nutrient cycling; ocean conditions and processes; spatial distribution patterns; waves and wave energy; *specific locations and lifeforms*

coastal geology, 14-31; ecological change and, 16; erosion, sediment transport, and their impacts, 18, 20, 81-82, 208; glacial cycles, 14-15, 18-19, 156, 201; mountain uplift, 19, 21; species diversity and, 21, 23, 30, 139-40, 202; subduction, 19, 21, 22; tectonic processes and coastal characteristics, 17-18, 19, 21-23, 22, 29-30, 186, 200-202; time scales, 16-17; volcanism and volcanic rock, 17, 18, 19, 22. *See also specific regions and locations*

coastal upwelling: causes and dynamics of, 23, 24-26, *25*, 27, 29, 46; ecosystem impacts, 25-26, 30, 45, 133, 186

coast redwood, 124

Codium: fragile, 67; *setchellii*, 166-67

coho salmon, 105, 106. *See also* salmon

coloration: color polymorphism, 131-32, 196-97, *197*; cryptic, 130, 178, 189-90, *190*; defensive bright coloration, 211, 218, *218*; green anemones, 77, 217-18; seaweeds and seagrasses, 39

Columbia River: geological history, 18, 151, 162; impacts on marine and estuarine conditions, 111, 133, 141, 142; maps, *111*, *149*; sea lions in, 230; sediments from, 110, 149

common murre, 153, *153*, 179

common names, 67

common tern, 182

competition, 49, 51-53, 62; for space, 51-52, *52*, 55, 60, 190

conservation and stewardship, 11

Coos Bay (OR), 156; map, *187*

coralline algae, 76, 125, 213-14; photos, 77, *116*, *152*, 205, *215*, *225*

cordgrasses, 134

Coriolis effect, 23-24, *24*, 25

cormorants, 153, 162, 173, 177

Corvus: brachyrhynchos, 182; *corax*, 182

Cottidae, 224, *225*

crabs: black-clawed, 209; Dungeness, 88, 133, *141*, 158, 209; feeding behavior, 58; habitat preferences, 29; hermit crabs, 115, 120, 128-29, *128*, 171, 209, 210; in Hood Canal, 88; invasive species, 54; kelp crabs, 88, *163*, 209; on the Oregon coast, *163*, 164, 166, 171, 207, 209, 210; parasitic barnacles and, 139; pea crabs, *87*, 174; porcelain, 209; shore crabs, 87, 127-28, *127*, 153, 209; on Washington's outer coast, 115, 116, 120, 128-29, *128*, 133, 153, 158. *See also* sand or mole crab

Crassostrea gigas, 54, 89, 100-101, *101*

Crepidula adunca, 204

crows, 142, 182

Cryptochiton stelleri, 221, *221*, 229

pine, shore, 151
pink salmon, 105, 106. *See also* salmon
pinnipeds. *See* sea lions; seals
Pinnixa, 174
Pinus contorta, 151
Pisaster ochraceus, 131-32, *131*, 196, 219
plainfin midshipman, 103-4
plankton, 26, 52, 56, 61
plants, 41, 44-45; dodder, 143; dune
  grass, 142; European beach grass,
  198, *198*; forest tree species, 124-25,
  151, 191; invasive plant species, 54,
  158, 198, *198*; pickleweed, 143, *143*;
  vs. algae and seaweeds, 134-35. *See
  also* seagrasses
plovers, 178; killdeer, 178; western
  snowy plover, 137, *137*, 142
polar bear, 59-60, 227
Polinices lewisii. See *Neverita lewisii*
Pollicipes polymerus, 129-30, *129*. *See
  also* gooseneck barnacles
polychaete worms, 87, 153, 164
porcelain crab, 209
Porichthys notatus, 103-4
porpoises, 173, 227-28
Port Angeles (WA), 112; map, *111*
Possession Sound, 78
Postelsia palmaeformis, 43-44, *44*,
  170-71
Potlatch State Park, 90
predation, 49, 55-60; competition for
  food, 52-53; defensive and offensive
  traits, 58-59; ecosystem impacts of,
  60, 227; feeding behaviors, 55-58;
  land-sea predation linkages and
  their impacts, 58, 59-60, 106-7,
  122, 124, 144; zonation and, 62-63,
  194, *213*. *See also* defensive traits;
  food webs; offensive traits; *specific
  lifeforms*
pricklebacks, 224-25
primary production, 44-45, 46, 61, 186.
  See also biological productivity

productivity. *See* biological
  productivity
Pseudotsuga menziesii, 124, 191
Ptilota filicina, 163, *164*
public coastal access rights, 150
Public Trust Doctrine, 150
puffin, tufted, 120, 180, 212
Puffinus griseus. See *Ardenna grisea*
Puget Sound and greater Salish
  Sea, 70-107; environment and
  ecology, 36, 70-72; invasive species,
  54, 85; maps, *9*, *71*; places to explore,
  72-90; public coastal access rights,
  150; salmon and salmon declines,
  105-7; species of interest, 90-105.
  *See also specific locations and
  lifeforms*
Pugettia, 88, 209; *producta*, *163*
purple olive snail, 164, *165*, 220, *220*
purple-ringed top snail, 65
purple shore crab, 127, *127*, 209
purple urchin, 67, 114, *172*
purple varnish clam, 54
Pyropia, 37
Pyrosoma, 96-97

raccoons, 58, 59, 164
Raja binoculata, 226
raven, common, 182
rays, 157, 226
razor clam, 140-41, *141*
red algae (seaweeds), 126, 134, 171,
  211, 214; *Ahnfeltiopsis*, 188, *189*;
  coralline algae, 76, 77, 116, 125, *152*,
  205, 213-14, *215*, 225; dulse, 74-75;
  Halosaccion glandiforme, 65, *66*,
  202-3, *204*; *Neorhodomela larix*,
  193, *194*; *Ptilota filicina*, 163, *164*;
  Schizymenia pacifica, 163; Turkish
  towel, 90; Turkish washcloth, 90
red-banded bamboo worm, 174
red sea urchin, 67
redwood, coast, 124

204, 210, 211; on Washington's outer coast, 114, 116, *116*, 118, *119*, 120, 128-29, *128*, 130, 142; whelks, 114, 116, *128*, 129-30, *197*, 210, *210*. *See also* limpets

snow goose, 181

snowy plover, western, 137, *137*, 142

sockeye salmon, 105, 106, *106*. *See also* salmon

sooty shearwater, 177

South Beach (San Juan Island, WA), 75-76

South Cove (Cape Arago State Park, OR), *201*

southern Oregon coast, 186-231; environment and ecology, 186-88, 230-31; maps, *9*, *187*; places to explore, 188-213; species of interest, 213-30. *See also specific locations*

southern Washington coast, 132-44; environment and ecology, 112; places to explore, *111*, 132-42; species of interest, 142-44. *See also specific locations*

South Slough National Estuarine Reserve (OR), 206-7

spaghetti worms, *87*

spatial distribution patterns: competition for space, 51-52, *52*, 55, 60, 190; disturbance and, 43, 44, 51, 52, *52*, 161, *161*, 168; spatial facilitation, 44, 49, 52, 60-61, 161; zonation, 62-63, *62*, 120, *194*, *213*. *See also specific lifeforms*

species diversity. *See* biotic diversity

sperm whale, 228

sponges, 95-96, *97*, 152-53, *152*, *160*, 211

spruce, Sitka, 125, 151, 191

stalked jellyfish, 81

starfish. *See* sea stars

Steller, Georg, 229

Steller sea lion, 78, 171, 205, 227, 229-30

Steller's sea cow, 227, 229

Sterna hirundo, 182

stipeless kelp. *See* sea cabbage

storm petrel, Leach's, 212

Strait of Juan de Fuca, 70, 78, 88; exploring the Salt Creek Recreation Area, 112-14; maps, *71*, *111*; northern elephant seal population, 229

Strawberry Hill (OR), 188, 191-95, *192*

Strongylocentrotus purpuratus, 67, 114, *172*

sunlight, 38-39, 44, 45. *See also* photosynthesis

Sunset Bay State Park (OR), 200

Sunset Beach (Cape Arago State Park, OR), 201

Sunset Beach (Tillamook Head, OR), 149; map, *149*

surfgrasses, 76, 112, *113*, 151, *152*, *203*, 211

surfperch, 223

surf smelt, 188, 225-26

suspension feeding, 55-56, 64, 85

swash and swash periods, 28, 63-64. *See also* waves and wave energy

Talitridae. *See* beach hoppers

tar spot algae, 50, 215

taxonomic nomenclature, 64-67

tectonic processes: coastal characteristics and, 17-18, 19, 21-23, *22*, 29-30, 186, 200-202; earthquakes and tsunamis, 19, 154, 155. *See also* volcanism and volcanic rock

Tegula, 128, 211; *funebralis*, 116, 203-4, 205, *210*

temperatures: heat and desiccation, 46, 48, *48*, 63; ocean temperatures and their impacts, 26, 29, 37, 38; temperature variations and microclimates, 37-38, 156-57

Terebellidae, *87*

tern, common, 182

threatened or endangered species: bald eagle, 117, 153, 177-78; brown pelican, 153, 177; marbled murrelet, 78, 120, 227; northern elephant seal, 171, 205, 228-29; orcas, 73, 104-5, *104*, 171, 173, 205; salmon as, 107, 230; western snowy plover, 137, *137*, 142; whale recoveries, 11, 228. *See also* extinctions

Three Capes Scenic Route (OR), 158-67

Threemile Beach (OR), 28

Thuja plicata, 124

tidal cycles, 35-37, *36*, 63. *See also* estuaries

tidepools, 8, 15, 39. *See also specific locations and lifeforms*

Tillamook Bay (OR), 156-58, *157*; map, *149*

Tillamook Head (OR), 149, 151; exploring the area, 151-54, 156; map, *149*

time scales, 16-17

top snails, 65, 210, *210*

toxins and toxic releases: chemical defenses, 59, 77, 117, 123, 126-27, 211, 218; chemical offensive traits, 56, 59, 93, 94, 98, 218; from seaweed decomposition, 92; toxic algal blooms, 220

tracks and sign, 164, *165*, 226

trees: driftwood and drift logs, 75, 81, 121-22, 124; forest tree species, 124-25, 151, 191

Tsuga heterophylla, 125

tsunamis, 154, 155

tube worms, 140, 152-53

tufted puffin, 120, 180, 212

tunicates, 95-97, *97*, 152-53, *152*, 211; invasive species, 85

turban snails, *116*, 128, 203-4, *204*, *210*, 211

Turkish towel, 90

Turkish washcloth, 90

Twanoh State Park (WA), 90

Ulva, 89, 91-92, *91*, 127, 134

Ulvaria obscura, 59

upwelling. *See* coastal upwelling

urchins. *See* sea urchins

Urechis caupo, 67

Uria aalge, 153, *153*, 179

Urile, 173, 177. *See also* cormorants

Vancouver, George, 70

Vancouver Island, 72-73

Velella, 94-95

Venerupis philippinarum, 53

volcanism and volcanic rock, 17, 18, 22; on the Oregon coast, 18, 19, 151, 154, 159, 162, 171, 188

Washington. *See* Puget Sound and greater Salish Sea

Washington's outer coast, 110-45; environment and ecology, 18, 110-12; exploring the northern coast, *111*, 112-22; exploring the southern coast, *111*, 132-42; headlands and sea stacks, 20, 118, *119*, 120, 141-42; maps, *9*, *111*; northern coast species of interest, 123-32; public access rights, 150; sea otter population, 230; southern coast species of interest, 142-44. *See also specific locations*

water quality: green tides and, 92; mussels and, 219-20

waves and wave energy: on the Oregon coast, 148, 151, 192; physical and ecosystem impacts of, 27-28, 40-44, 45, 63-64, 80-81; tides as waves, 35; tsunamis, 154, 155; winds and, 27, 46. *See also* disturbance and exposure

weather, 21, 26-27, 29-30. *See also* climate; temperatures; winds and wind patterns

western gull, 153, 178-79

western hemlock, 125, 191

western red cedar, 124

ABOUT THE AUTHORS

RYAN P. KELLY is an associate professor at the University of Washington's School of Marine and Environmental Affairs, working on topics ranging from marine biology to genetics to environmental law and policy. He has always wanted to be a marine biologist. A native of California, he lives in Seattle and loves the diversity of life along the West Coast. He previously worked at Stanford University and holds degrees from the University of California, Los Angeles (BS), Columbia University (PhD), and UC Berkeley (JD).

TERRIE KLINGER is a marine ecologist specializing in the nearshore biota of the US West Coast. Drawn to seaweeds and the animals that live among them, she has studied intertidal systems from Alaska to Mexico. The author of scientific publications and recipient of a handful of professional awards, she is happiest when counting snails on the beach at low tide. She obtained her PhD from the Scripps Institution of Oceanography. A professor at the University of Washington for more than two decades, she lives and teaches in Seattle and Friday Harbor.

Raised on the shores of the Pacific Ocean, **JOHN J. MEYER**'s earliest memories are connected to salt water. He has degrees in environmental studies from University of California, Santa Barbara (BA) and zoology from University of New Hampshire (MS) and has studied invertebrate ecology along the US West Coast and the deep sea of the Gulf of Maine. He has also worked on ocean policy at local, state, and national levels, which included time as a fellow in the US House of Representatives. Meyer currently is a communications coach and trainer at the University of Washington College of the Environment, helping scientists share their work with the wider world.